Bargain Hunting
in Greater New York

How to Order:

Quantity discounts are available from the publisher, Prima Publishing, P.O. Box 1260RLB, Rocklin, CA 95677; telephone (916) 624-5718. On your letterhead include information concerning the intended use of the books and the number of books you wish to purchase.

U.S. Bookstores and Libraries: Please submit all orders to St. Martin's Press, 175 Fifth Avenue, New York, NY 10010; telephone (212) 674-5151.

Bargain Hunting
in Greater New York

RICHARD LAERMER

Prima Publishing
P.O. Box 1260RLB
Rocklin, CA 95677
(916) 624-5718

Copy Editing by Amy Pattullo
Typography by Recorder Typesetting Network
Production by Robin Lockwood, Bookman Productions
Interior design by Renee Deprey
Cover design by The Dunlavey Studio

Prima Publishing
Rocklin, CA

Library of Congress Cataloging-in-Publication Data
Laermer, Richard, 1960–
    Bargain hunting in Greater New York/Richard Laermer.
        p.   cm.
    Includes index.
    ISBN 1-55958-030-5
    1. Shopping—New York Region—Guide-books. 2. New
York Region—Description and travel—Guide-books.   1. Title.
TX336.5.N482N475 1990
380.1'45'000257471—dc20   90-36217
                                                                         CIP

90 91 92 93 — 10 9 8 7 6 5 4 3 2 1

Printed in the United States of America

To Lou and Gloria Laermer
Who Taught Me the Meaning
of a Bargain

A PAEAN TO THE NEW YORK AREA

by unknown

New York is noisy
New York is overcrowded
New York is ugly
New York is unhealthy
New York is outrageously expensive
New York is bitterly cold in winter
New York is steaming hot in summer
I wouldn't live outside New York
for anything in the world

February 21, 1925
The New Yorker
Price 15 cents

CONTENTS

	Introduction	ix
1	Shoes	1
2	Comprehending the Districts	9
3	Sample Sales—"Never Shop a Department Store Again!"	17
4	Flea Markets	23
5	Shop-by-Mail	30
6	New Jersey	38
7	Best of Orchard Street	45
8	Brooklyn the Eclectic	51
9	Downtown Brooklyn and Flatbush	59
10	Upstate World	68
11	Outerwear	74
12	Menswear	81
13	Womenswear	93
14	Children's Wear	104
15	Cosmetics and Perfumes	110
16	Jewelry Ideas	120
17	Stationery and Household Items	127
18	Luggage and Carry-Alls	136
19	Furniture	143
20	Home Appliances	156
21	Services and Unusual Bargains	168

22 Novelties and Gift Items 178
23 Those Answered Questions 185
24 Transitional Blocks 194
25 Unnoticed Areas 198
ACKNOWLEDGMENTS 204
INDEX 205
COUPONS

INTRODUCTION

DOING MY HOMEWORK

Rummaging through a store along with my handy tape recorder, I was suddenly interrupted by a menacing security guard. "What are you doing?" he wondered. I thought it was obvious: I was taking verbal notes on the store's selection, price, and atmosphere. For a second it looked as though he might assault me. Then he shook his head and smiled.

"So what do you think?"

That was the story of my life for a year, as I expanded and double-checked research begun four years earlier lecturing groups on how to shop New York. As a New York-based reporter I'm always learning as much as I can about the city and its environs, figuring out ways to share my findings with residents and visitors. After I wrote *Native's Guide to New York: 750 Ways to Have the Time of Your Life in the City*, I realized that most people don't have the time to compare bargains all over the tri-state area, and I set out to collect helpful hints to make informed shopping easier.

And shopping is definitely a job. At each block, mall, or outlet center I visited while writing this book, I had to find a different way to shop effectively. The smart shopper has to know where bargains are placed; when a store has its special sales; what racks to stay away from; and which stores are absolute no-goes for the bargain hunter. More crucially, you have to know the language: "sample sale," "stock sale," "clearance," "surplus store," "closeout," and the venerable phrase "going out of business" are all key terms in the shopping vernacular.

Then I began to discover ways in which to talk to shop owners, street vendors, clerks, and stock people, to find out which brands are rip-offs, when the big sales are, and even which other stores have better buys. (You would be surprised how many salespeople will steer you to a better-equipped store if they like you.)

Lastly, I learned about the tables—given on the following pages—of helpful information about seasons, addresses, sale days, sizes, and other data on how to use the stores of New York City's five boroughs, Long Island, upstate New York, New Jersey, and Connecticut. Pore over this book and takes notes on stores that intrigue you; the information included will make it easy to discern where, when, how, and *if* you should go.

Please: When you find yourself impressed or intrigued with a store, outlet center, factory warehouse, sidewalk vendor, phone or mail-order service, or sample sale, be sure to patronize that vendor as often as possible. This way you help prevent being hit with the numbing news that it isn't in business any longer. Every store owner needs faithful customers, which is one reason I'm glad to present information on what makes certain stores and services such good buys.

And at the very end of this book, I have included coupons to give you an additional incentive to purchase from these special sellers.

STOCK 'EM UP

You will find extensive explanations of shopper's jargon throughout the pages of *Bargain Hunting*. Every now and then the buying term "stocking up" comes into play. This is an important one in bargain hunting. It means that a particular store, warehouse center, outlet, or showroom has such low prices—and offers such terrific products—that it's worth your while to walk out with tons of whatever is being sold! Pay attention to those places; if you plan on stopping by, bring a car, U-Haul, Mack truck, or half a dozen friends to help cart all the amazing purchases home.

Many of the coupons in the book are for "stocking up" locations. For those you have an even greater incentive to visit already low-priced establishments—to save even more money with pages of generous offers in the back.

WHAT'S IN SEASON

Here's a calendar used by department stores and boutiques, showing the selling seasons and dates on which they place the newest fashions on the selling floor. If you are interested in getting new styles as soon as they are produced, these are some dates to keep in mind. For shoppers who are true bargain connoisseurs, however, remember that big sales occur around sixty days after the merchandise is put out. Called the "season price break," those days are the only time you should ever rush to a department store.

SPRING I   January 1
SPRING II (SUMMER)   January 15
FALL I   June 1
FALL II (WINTER)   July 1
TRANSITION   September 1
HOLIDAY I (CRUISEWEAR)   November 1
HOLIDAY II (DRESS-UP)   December 1

See chapter 23, "Those Answered Questions," for more information on how to use department stores. See below for addresses in the five boroughs of these multilevel emporiums.

SHOP BY DEPARTMENT

Since shopping department stores isn't the greatest

way to save money, the big stores aren't covered at great length in these pages. As the book constantly demonstrates, you can do better in a small store or boutique than you can at a Macy's or Bloomingdale's. Here, however, is the basic information for the department stores since they do carry the newest works of most fashion designers. Except for Alexander's, this group sells top designs at the highest price until the "storewide sale" days when department managers give customers a welcome reduction in price.

Abraham & Straus (A&S) Sixth Avenue & 33rd Street, 594-8500

Abraham & Straus (A&S) of Brooklyn 420 Fulton Street at Fulton Mall, 718/875-7200

Abraham & Straus (A&S) of Queens 90-15 Queens Boulevard Elmhurst, 718/271-7200

Alexander's Lexington Avenue & 58th Street, 593-0880

Alexander's of Bronx Bruckner Boulevard, Tiffany Street and the Grand Concourse/Fordham Road, 365-2020

Alexander's of Brooklyn Kings Plaza in Mill Basin, 718/253-1212

Barney's 106 Seventh Avenue, 929-9000

Bendel's 10 West 57th Street, 247-1100

Bergdorf Goodman Fifth Avenue & 57th Street, 753-7300

Bloomingdale's Third Avenue & 59th Street, 705-2000

Macy's Broadway & 34th Street, 695-4400

Macy's of Brooklyn 1101 Flatbush Avenue in Flatbush, 718/856-5000; Kings Plaza in Mill Basin, 718/253-3100

Saks Fifth Avenue Fifth Avenue & 50th Street, 753-4000

Sears Roebuck of Bronx 400 East Fordham Road in Fordham Plaza, 295-3200

Sears Roebuck of Brooklyn Bedford Avenue & Beverley Road in Flatbush, 718/469-8000

Many of the above have branches in upstate New York, New Jersey, and Connecticut.

EASY ADDRESS CHART OF MANHATTAN

Follow this chart to figure out cross-streets in Manhattan: Take the number of the address, cancel the last figure, divide by 2, and *add or subtract* the key number below.

Avenue A: Add 3
Avenue B: Add 3
Avenue C: Add 3
Avenue D: Add 3
First Avenue: Add 3
Second Avenue: Add 3
Third Avenue: Add 10
Fourth Avenue: Add 4
Fifth Avenue—Up to #200: Add 13
 Up to #400: Add 16
 Up to #600: Add 18
 Up to #775: Add 20
 From #775 to #1286: Cancel the last figure and
 subtract 18
 Up to #1500: Add 45
 Above #2000: Add 24
Sixth Avenue: Subtract 12
Seventh Avenue—Up to #1800: Add 12
 Above #1800: Add 20
Eighth Avenue: Add 10
Ninth Avenue: Add 13
10th Avenue: Add 14
Amsterdam Avenue: Add 60
Audubon Avenue: Add 165
Broadway (#750 is 8th Street)

From #756 to #846: Subtract 29
From #847 to #953: Subtract 25
Above #953: Subtract 31
Columbus Avenue: Add 60
Convent Avenue: Add 127
Central Park West: Divide address by 10 and add 60
Edgecombe Avenue: Add 134
Fort Washington Avenue: Add 158
Lenox Avenue: Add 110
Lexington Avenue: Add 22
Madison Avenue: Add 26
Manhattan Avenue: Add 100
Park Avenue: Add 35
Pleasant Avenue: Add 101
Riverside Drive to 165th Street: Divide address by 10 and add 72
Nicholas Avenue: Add 110
Wadsworth Avenue: Add 173
West End Avenue: Add 60
York Avenue: Add 4

SIZE CHARTS FOR MEN, WOMEN, AND CHILDREN

WOMEN

Misses Dresses, Coats, Suits, and Skirts

US & UK	8	10	12	14	16	18
Europe	38	40	42	44	46	48

Junior Dresses

US & UK	7	9	11	13	15
Europe	34	36	38	40	42

Blouses and Sweaters

US & UK	30	32	34	36	38
Europe	38	40	42	44	46

Stockings

US & UK	8	8½	9	9½	10	10½
Europe	35	36	37	38	39	40

Shoes

US	5	6	7	8	9
UK	3½	4½	5½	6½	7½
Europe	35	36	38	38½	40

MEN

Suits, overcoats, sweaters, and pajamas

US & UK	34	36	38	40	42	44
Europe	44	46	48	50	52	54

Shirts

US & UK	14	14½	15	15½	16	16½	17
Europe	36	37	38	39	40	41	42

Shoes

US	8	8½	9	9½	10	10½	11
UK	7½	8	8½	9	9½	10	10½
Europe	41	42	43	43	44	44	45

Socks

US & UK	9½	10	10½	11	11½	12	12½
Europe	39	40	41	42	43	44	45

CHILDREN

US	2	4	6	8	10	12
Europe	40-45	50-55	60-65	70-75	80-85	90-95

THE YEAR IN SALE DAYS

January: White sales
February: Large appliances, bedding
March: Children's, men's clothing
April: Easter sales on clothing and especially hats
May: Lingerie
June: Pre-vacation boys' clothing, men's and women's underwear
July: Sportswear, shoes, men's summer suits

August: Furs, furniture, floor coverings, linens, hot
   weather goods, air conditioners, gardening tools
September: Housewares
October: Hosiery, lingerie, and costume jewelry
November: Early Christmas closeouts, men's shoes
December: *Caveat emptor.* Except in rare instances,
   nothing is on sale before Christmas.

Every effort has been made to ensure that all listings
in this book are accurate and up-to-date. But call before
you go—bargain places tend to be the first to go out of
business. And chain stores open and shut down branches
all the time. Check your local phone book.

All addresses are in Manhattan unless otherwise
stated. All phone numbers are in area code 212 unless
otherwise noted. (Bronx code will be 907 sometime in
1991).

CHAPTER 1

Shoes!

FELLMAN LTD.
24 East 44th Street and 102 Fulton Street
687-6788 and 227-0012
American Express, MC, Visa
Closed Sunday

Brands here include Bally, Bostonian, and French Shriner. This is a store where a man can go and be assured a shoe for between $80 and $100, and find classic brushed calf Oxfords selling for $150, 35 percent less than the Bally stores sell them for uptown. At this branch, located right off Nassau Street, you can find a sturdy selection of shoes at a decent price; the deals aren't incredible, but you can shop here with confidence. The uptown location is a little more like the famed and austere Eggers & Silk shoe shop, whose name it used to bear.

Get on the Fellman mailing list, because they have end-of-season sales that will either knock, or get, your socks off.

WEISS & MAHONEY
142 Fifth Avenue
675-1915
American Express, MC, Visa

Their catalogue is filled with the best selection of sneakers available, all at a fraction of the cost found anywhere else. Though nearby **Runner's World** (275 Seventh Avenue, 691-2565, closed Sundays, credit cards) carries the best of the fashionable brands, such as Nike and Reebok—see **The Athlete's Foot** below—here you will run into all the lowbrow brands—Keds, New Balance, and NoBrands. This is a store that specializes in what is called "camouflage" wear, and most of its stock is below market price. See chapter 12, "Menswear."

DUNHAM
P.O. Box 813, Brattleboro, VT 05302
800/843-2668; in Vermont, call 800/544-4202
American Express, MC, Visa

Dunham's has great buys for those willing to shop by mail: the best outdoor footwear at nearly 40 percent below retail purchases. There's great quality in the Dunham name, so if you want waterproof work boots, hiking shoes, leather boat shoes, or just regular old walking shoes, this is the place to turn to. Call for a free catalogue. See chapter 5, "Shop-by-Mail."

CHANDLERS
One World Trade Center
939-1449
American Express, MC, Visa

This is one of those chain stores you find in every city: great women's shoes are here at a fraction of regular retail prices. This is a very good place for brides who want to stock up for their wedding parties. You won't have trouble finding anything here; look for name brands

Cesare Paciotti, Testoni, Stephane Kelian, and even espadrilles and fashionable "combat boots" from Britain.

WHOLESALER'S SHOE OUTLET
Industrial Park at 20 Aquarian Drive, Secaucus NJ
(right off Enterprise Avenue South, off Route 3)
201/864-2136
MC, Visa
Closed Sunday

Here's a great place to find shoes for men and women at prices that have been cut by nearly 25 percent. These include Nunn Bush, Rockports, Dexter's, Clark's, Bally, Bostonian, and even the ones named after football player Roger Staubach. It's hard to find—in the back by Fashion Mate—but the nine-year-old branch is a fine place to stock up on shoes. Fairly large in size and staffed by nice people who manage and own the warehouse, Wholesaler's is Secaucus's best shoe deal. See chapter 6, "New Jersey."

99 X
210 East Sixth Street
460-8599
American Express

Next door to the East Village's ancient record shop "99," this is the best "rock-and-roll" shoe store for women. It's famous for eccentric shoes, mostly from England, and includes a hard-core selection of avant-garde fashions from local designers. The locals don't charge much for their experiments; they can start as low as $40.

RICHIE'S CHILDREN'S SHOES
183 Avenue B
228-5442
American Express, MC, Visa
Closed Wednesday

At first you might wonder why anyone would come

down to this neighborhood to shop. But once you enter the store, it's clear: Buster Browns, Stride Rite, Keds, and Blue Star all sell for about 50 percent less than at other stores (though only 20 percent less on newer items). The salespeople are honest about their selection—"We stock what we can get." And it's the right place to bring kids whose feet continue to grow. They also have some great Little Capezios—for little yuppies—and styles for pre-walkers, sizes one and two. Teens have fun here.

Why is Richie closed Wednesdays? Because that's when he goes looking for closeouts in children's shoes. If you can wait, their biggest sales take place in May.

CARLSEN IMPORT
524 Broadway, 3rd Floor
431-5940

Here you will find everything for the athlete, in a third-floor walkup. This wholesaler has sporting discounts on Adidas—older models selling at 75 percent off—Spaulding, Saucony, Osaga (and Osaga sports clothing too). Discounts are generally 30 percent off list price. Don't go on Saturday, for then it's much too crowded for any shopper. And that's the day when school groups come to look.

JOHN'S SHOE STORE
204 West 14th Street
255-7035
American Express, MC, Visa

There are no name brands here whatsoever—only the brands John gets from suppliers, and he won't tell anyone who they are. But for around $50 you can get throwaway shoes for men that are amazing, such as Viking "kick-arounds" that many men like because they are so shiny and comfortable. He stocks a few designers when he can get them, but don't bet on it. This is not the fanciest shop, but you may find you come here often.

WEST EIGHTH STREET SHOE STORES
Eighth Street between Fifth and Sixth Avenues

Although they have no proof, residents swear that Imelda Marcos was born on West Eighth Street, where there are over 15 shoe stores to look at (see below, "Orchard Street Redux," for another example of this phenomenon). Anywhere else it is tough to find, en masse, good women's shoes at a reasonable price.

In these stores all selections are basically from the same designers. So you'll want to go to the best and easiest to deal with: Village Cobbler (#60, 673-8530) and Sweet Feet (#38, 533-5947) for women; and Ritz Shoe Store (#14, 228-5377) for men.

However, be aware that chain stores from another borough will come to a strip like this merely to capitalize on its fame: Plaza on Eighth (#35, 477-4888) is an example. Compare each store; since they offer the same stock, prices can vary greatly.

NEW YORK SHOE COMPANY
489 Third Avenue
685-4056
American Express, MC, Visa, checks

Wow. Here is the best selection of women's and men's shoes in the city, with names like Cole-Haan, Ciro Bisanti, Linea Aldo, Gardini, Versace, Van Eli, Sesto Meucci, Mosaic, Aldo, and Mario Bruni. Also, ladies' summer sales are tremendous—shoes start at $20. It's a perfect shopping experience for shoe lovers because you usually save 20 percent off list price on everything!

MINNETONKA
P.O. Box 444, Bronx
365-7033

Here is another good mail-order idea: moccasins, loafers, and chukka boots that are very popular in these parts. You can order the free Minnetonka catalogue, and check out the many designs and the types of soles—crepe, boat, soft, polyurethane, even small soles for children. They carry both men's and women's sizes, at 20 percent below what's selling in the stores. Shipment is prompt. See chapter 5, "Shop-by-Mail."

ORMONT SHOES
59 Fourth Avenue
674-1600
MC, Visa

Now you're shopping at a women's shoe store that sells Evins, Golo, Geller, and Pailzzio, sizes five to ten. There are very few in stock that aren't of the highest quality, and that's only one reason why you should visit Ormont. The other is a discount that starts at 20 percent at the beginning of each season and goes to as high as 70 percent by season's end. A pretty store, Ormont caters to upscale buyers who want comfortable shoes on credit. Note that the store's slight facade makes it difficult to locate.

ATHLETE'S FOOT
1089 Lexington Avenue, 861-3700; 387 Avenue of the Americas, 627-2091; 16 West 57th Street, 586-1936; 34 East 8th Street, 260-0750; 1031 Third Avenue, 223-8022; 151 East 86th Street, 876-3200; 18 West 125th Street; 739 Third Avenue, 697-7870; 149 West 72nd Street, 874-1003; 2341 Broadway, 496-1919; 1890 Broadway, 757-5040
Also in the Bronx, Brooklyn, New Jersey, Connecticut and upstate New York

This chain specializes in providing runners with

everything they need and want: Nike, Adidas, New Balance, Brooks, and Reeboks, from $20 when big sales are on to $105 when sales are off. They will also resole old shoes at low prices, and they sell an uncannily large line of running suits. If you are athletically inclined, visit bulletin boards that list sporting events at the front of the stores.

FRANKEL'S DISCOUNT STORE (FOR BOOTS)

See chapter 7, "Brooklyn the Eclectic."

EXTRAS

I didn't want to end this chapter without reminding readers that shoes are a difficult item to buy inexpensively so shoppers must look hard to find good buys. The **Stapleton Shoe** counter (68 Trinity Place, back of Trinity Church, 964-6329) has been selling all sizes of the casual comfort shoe Dexter for $48! And women can hit the **Hot Shoes** shop (208 West 38th Street, 730-1042), for regularly held "renovation sales" of espadrilles, sandals, and kickback shoes for $40–$90. Women can find a mail-order bonus of the (advertised) "coolest shoes on earth," meaning real alligator shoes, for just $12.95 through **Archie McPhee and Company** (P.O. Box 30852, Seattle, WA 98111, 206/547-2467). Also for women, espadrille pumps go for around $25 through FM Accessories (126 Ludlow Street, 673-3230). **Leslie's Bootery** (319 Grand Street, 431-9196) has fine selections of Bass and Bally boots, in addition to whatever they can get their hands on, at a discount of 20–30 percent. **Sherman Shoes** (121 Division Street, 233-7898), which for nearly a century has advertised fine men's shoes and boots with discounts as high as 70 percent on last year's Ballys, now has added ladies' low-priced shoes. Lastly, the Lower East Side's **M & M Shoe Center** (302 Grand Street, 966-2702) has two floors of designer names at mid-price for men and women. They have no closeout sales but will order in your size whatever they display. These stores take American Express, MC, and Visa; all the stores close Sunday, except Leslie's, Sherman, and M & M, which close Saturday.

ORCHARD STREET REDUX

Women can start a shopping spree with a walk around Orchard Street, New York City's original shoe mart. You can spend an afternoon at the following shoe shops and find yourself walking away with tremendous buys. Most are closed on Saturday.

- Charles S. Cohen & Sons, 31 Orchard, 925-3996
- Giorgiolini, 51 Orchard, 226-3736
- Orchard Bootery, 75 Orchard, 966-0688
- Accessories Arcade, 95 Orchard, 226-6036
- Lace-Up, 110 Orchard, 475-8040—see chapter 6, "Best of Orchard Street"
- Jolie Madame, 145 Orchard, 477-2471
- John Cipriano, 148 Orchard, 477-5858
- The City Athlete, 131, 132A, 132B, 135, and 163 Orchard, 982-0840
- J & H Katz, 167 Orchard, 477-3777
- G & B Sneaker Center, 184 Orchard, 260-3184

Now that your feet are feeling fine, start shopping.

CHAPTER 2

Comprehending the Districts

Shopping in Manhattan takes patience. Sometimes, however, finding an area's trends is what it takes. In Manhattan, unlike most cities, there are districts made for shopping in: if you can recognize them, you can go from store to store along a single street seeing the best of whatever you're looking for. These are places perfect for bargain-hunters; if you find the right area, you're sure to find what you need at a good price. If you're not satisfied with *any* shop in a district, keep looking; there may be other pockets elsewhere. Try to memorize the following list of New York hints. Or rip out these pages to stick on your refrigerator!

CDS, TAPES, AND RECORDS

Tower Records (692 and 1965 Broadway, 505-1500) is the best for selection. Then again, West Eighth Street, along University Place and Sixth Avenue, is where the cheapest new and second-hand record shops are. The same trend continues on St. Marks Place (East Eighth Street).

PERFUMES AND COLOGNES

The best quality can be found on 17th Street between Broadway and Sixth Avenue. Here you will undoubtedly see brand name and off-brand fragrant water, including sample bottles at very low prices. They also sell newfangled versions of famous scents—inexpensive "facsimile" perfumes. Look for places marked "wholesale" that will sell small quantities to walk-in buyers. See chapter 15, "Cosmetics and Perfumes."

DRUGSTORE CENTRAL

Along Broadway below 72nd Street are a slew of drugstores that sell all the non-pharmaceutical items such as bathroom supplies and household goods. Discounts are sometimes 40 percent off regular retail prices. These are stock-up stores, places you go to get things in large supply. See chapter 15, "Cosmetics and Perfumes."

DINERS

The best cheap places to eat are where the truck drivers are. Go to the west-side strip, which is West Street or 12th Avenue, and see the diners with names like Market and Main.

FURS

Look around the garment district, where a good deal can be found in the upper 20s and lower 30s until 38th Street. You will see the warehouses and distribution centers that are meant for fur-lovers. The best fur block is undoubtedly West 28th Street between Seventh and Eighth Avenues. It's a good retail street, hosting several showrooms that are only open weekdays. See chapter 11, "Outerwear."

LIGHTING

The Bowery from East Seventh Street to Chinatown's Chatham Square is considered a mini lighting town. For more details, see chapter 20, "Furniture." Also, lighting specials can be found on Second Avenue, in the upper 60s and throughout the 70s. This area has a good number of lighting supply shops. See chapter 20, "Home Appliances."

PLANTS AND FLOWERS

Sixth Avenue from West 23rd Street to West 29th Street is the main Manhattan plant district. If you visit at approximately 6 a.m. you will get the best deals. Maybe the early bird gets his fern? See chapter 21, "Services and Unusual Bargains."

ANTIQUE AND SECOND-HAND CLOTHING

Lower Broadway from East 14th to Houston Streets will make a perfect pit-stop for old clothes. Then a few blocks lower, just below Spring Street, you can go to **Alice Underground,** the best place for second-hand men's shirts, sweaters, and scarves. See chapter 12, "Menswear."

THRIFT SHOPS FOR CLOTHING

Thrifts are where neighborhood residents go to unload their old belongings; the monies garnered usually go to charity. In the 70s on and off Third Avenue there are thrift shops that sell whatever local residents wish to be rid of. In this ritzy area, that merchandise is pretty good! See chapter 12, "Menswear."

JEWELRY

Nowhere in the United States will you locate more reputable jewelry dealers than on West 47th Street between Fifth and Eighth Avenues. See chapter 16, "Jewelry Ideas."

ANTIQUES

Antiques abound on University Place, Broadway, and Fourth Avenue, between East 14th and East 9th Streets. There is an expensive collection of shops called **Manhattan Art and Antiques,** nestled inside a giant building at 1050 Second Avenue, where normally expensive stores often have decent closeouts. Also, Greenwich Avenue between Seventh and Eighth Avenues is home to several fine antiqueries. Lastly, there's East 11th Street. See chapter 19, "Furniture."

HANDBAGS

West 26th and West 27th Streets between Fifth and Sixth Avenues are recognized as Handbag Central. These two blocks are crammed with small handbag, purse, and wallet shops. See chapter 18, "Luggage and Carry-Alls."

HOME APPLIANCES

See the Lower East Side for small appliances. It's not a good idea to ask the clerks about the newest gadgets— they don't truly comprehend them. So if you're looking for high tech, forget these places. However, old-fashioned merchandise—egg beaters, hot plates—are stocked high here. And you can do well if you know how to haggle. See chapter 20, "Home Appliances."

PHOTO DISTRICTS

This area, now known as the Flatiron District, is from 14th Street to 23rd Street on either side of Fifth Avenue. It contains vendors who love to talk price, and used camera stores, which are now called "photo exchanges."

Also, find camera stores galore in the upper west 30s. See chapter 20, "Home Appliances."

THEATERS (BROADWAY)

"Broadway" is seventeen blocks in the 40s and 50s right off of Broadway (the Great White Way). There are many ways to get cheap tickets. For the scoop, see chapter 23, "Those Answered Questions."

I can't resist telling you what a wonderful party you'll participate in if you walk along West 45th Street in midtown at around 10:15 p.m. That's when the shows let out, and people excitedly pour out of the theaters. Don't miss it!

THEATERS (OFF-BROADWAY)

There is no Off-Broadway district, per se. Though if you are willing to take chances, you could try the East Village theaters, from Houston to 14th Street, off Third, Second, and First Avenues. That is truly the home for today's experimental companies. See Introduction.

GARMENT CENTER

Below 34th Street, which is where Seventh Avenue

gets most congested, you will find the so-called "garmentos" on each side street. See chapter 13, "Womenswear."

FABRICS

The lower thirties, off Seventh Avenue, is fabric heaven. See chapter 13, "Womenswear."

GOOD JUNK

Take a trek along Canal Street, peering inside each door. Then be sure to see the *tschachkes* outside, in bins. Try not to take Canal Street products seriously except if buying electronic parts and so-called gag gifts.

BOOKS

Once Fourth Avenue below 14th Street was New York's famed book haven. At the remaining store, **Pageant Books** at Ninth Street and Fourth Avenue, the management tells fascinating tales. Today all of Fifth Avenue is book heaven. Go to 18th Street where **Barnes & Nobles** has three major stores—one used books, one brand-new offerings, and one specializing in children's readers. The nearest side street is a browser's paradise: 18th Street between Fifth and Sixth Avenues. Also, find used and rare book stores along Fifth Avenue in the 50s and 60s. See chapter 25, "Unnoticed Areas."

FISH MARKET

Fulton Market off the South Street Seaport is a good place to buy fresh fish, especially since the men unfurl their wares from right out of the nets (962-1608). See chapter 22, "Novelties and Gift Items."

"FUNKY CLOTHING" STORES

East Village: those blocks off Avenue A have great buys on odd clothes. East Seventh Street has fun accessory shops and a wild, unexpected card boutique. See chapter 12, "Menswear."

CAFES AND COFFEE-KLATSCHES

Such places, which sell mainly coffees, cakes, and tiny sandwiches, are slowly becoming extinct. What's left of them can be found in the West Village: MacDougal Street, Sullivan Street, Thompson Street, and LaGuardia Place just above Houston Street.

JEWISH FOOD AND JEWISH ARTIFACTS

Find these on Grand Street, Essex Street, and Hester Street, all on the eastern side of Canal Street. See chapter 21, "Services and Unusual Bargains," and chapter 25, "Unnoticed Areas."

OUTDOOR STREET SELLERS

The best sidewalk salespeople are on lower Broadway; clothing marketeers set up shop along the avenue between Houston and 14th Streets. Recently I also spotted reputable street salespeople hanging portable shingles along Fifth between 38th and 57th Streets. You can find fine art, books, bolo ties, costume jewelry, knickknacks, and toys at some of these fly-by-night operations. See chapter 21, "Services and Unusual Bargains."

ONE-DAY UNADVERTISED SALES EVENTS

Macy's has great one-day sales events nearly every

month. Being that it *is* the world's largest department store, it's the one with the largest mailing list. Get yourself on it if you want to be notified of their special sales. See Introduction.

Sample Sales— "Never Shop a Department Store Again!"

How can you acquire things for little money without entering a store? Just go to "sample sales," or "stock sales," which do not offer samples but leftover brand-new merchandise. Designers, manufacturers, dealers, wholesalers, and garment center officials hold these clearances when merchandise accumulates in warehouses.

Usually it means that too much stock was manufactured. Designers and manufacturers often ship items to stores too late and the goods are therefore returned to them. Or, in some cases, a designer or distributor discovers there's an overrun of last year's models still hanging around. So, with strictly word-of-mouth advertising, they invite shoppers to purchase the surplus men's and women's clothing, furs, kid's stuff, jewelry, health and beauty items, even furniture, at so-called sample sales.

Elysa Lazar, publisher of the **S & B Report,** the only publication dedicated to sample sale and wholesale/warehouse shopping (679-5400, $40 a year; see coupon in back), explains that in the '90s sample sales have entered a new era.

There was a time when people thought of shopping in a warehouse or showroom as shoddy. Nowadays, though it's pretty difficult to predict when these sales will occur, the stigma is no longer, and you may never want to leave a sample sale once you discover it. The catches are: you usually can't try anything on, and cash is often the only form of payment accepted (but note exceptions to these rules).

Be careful, Lazar says. A bargain's a bargain only if you use what you buy. If it only sits in your closet, you will have wasted your money just as if you'd spent too much.

Here are some of the most dependable full-time sample sales:

SIMPLY SAMPLES
150 West 36th Street, 3rd Floor
268-0448
MC, Visa
Closed Sunday

For fifteen years this garment district staple has bought designer overruns, sometimes ordering them on consignment from the makers. New inventory arrives constantly, and everything in stock sells for $50 or *less.* All womenswear items are here, including outerwear. Original wholesale prices were $40–$249 and are now selling from $20 to $50. Additional seasonal merchandise can be found, all from famous designers, all imported from Europe. Try-ons are always permitted. See chapter 13, "Womenswear."

EXECUTIVE APPAREL
110 West 46th Street, 2nd Floor
719-0470
Closed Saturday and Sunday

This is sample-sale expert Elysa Lazar's favorite place to shop. "Well-made separates and open all the time" is the slogan of Executive Apparel, which calls itself the perfect place for the '90s woman. Strong suits, jackets, pants, skirts, blouses, and topcoats will take you from the office to that nighttime party. Fabrics are the finest silks, 100% wool, gabardine, and cool wool to be worn all year, all in subtle shades. Sizes 4–14 are available, and try-ons are permitted. See chapter 13, "Womenswear."

FENN WRIGHT & MANSON
500 Seventh Avenue, 11th Floor
704-9922
American Express, MC, Visa
Closed Saturday through Tuesday

You can always find the best of the Fall, Early Spring, and Holiday seasonal collections here. There are sarong skirts, nauticals, navy, red, and animal prints. Men's silk shirts, too, but mostly womenswear. Buy someone a great cotton sweater in this well-decorated warehouse of sample bargains. Prices are $5–$25. Try-ons are permitted. See chapter 13, "Womenswear."

OMANTI
530 Seventh Avenue, 9th Floor
302-0555
American Express, MC, Visa
Closed Saturday and Sunday

Omanti sells last season's items at wholesale prices (if it's fall, then it must be summer at Omanti). You will find women's clothing here, including skirts, blouses, palazzo and wool gabardine pants, and much more. Try-ons are not permitted. See chapter 13, "Womenswear."

ST. MARTIN
498 Seventh Avenue, 20th Floor
279-2211
Closed Saturday and Sunday

St. Martin carries high-fashion women's clothing, including dresses for special occasions. Costume designers buy clothing here. Sales feature sequins, jersey, silk, lace, hand-beaded tops, and tank dresses, as well as one-of-a-kind samples. Sizes 4–14, petite, regular, and large sizes 1X-3X are available. Prices are wholesale, $60–$600. Try-ons are permitted. See chapter 13, "Womenswear."

JONE SCHIFRIN
389 Fifth Avenue, Room 709
685-6806
Closed Saturday and Sunday

At this writing, jone (sic) is as fashionable as the T.V. show "thirtysomething." Her jewelry is unpretentious, however, and that includes earrings, pairs and singles, necklaces, pins, or any odd jewel, including "irreplaceable" settings. The back room has cash-and-carry bargains. Note: as Valentine's Day approaches, prices are lowered daily! See chapter 16, "Jewelry Ideas."

AVIREX FACTORY
33-00 47th Avenue
Falchi Building, Long Island City
718/482-1997
Checks accepted
Closed Sunday

Avirex is known for designing the popular leather

bomber jackets, or "distressed" leather. They sell here for 50 percent off retail prices. You can also find sheepskin, nylon, and cotton offerings—hundreds in stock at all times at this huge warehouse. There's no better quality at these prices anywhere. Try-ons are permitted. Sales are held at 1466 Broadway, a popular building for sample sales. See chapter 11, "Outerwear."

GOLDIN FELDMAN FURS
345 Seventh Avenue, 12th Floor
594-4415
American Express, MC, Visa

This exceptionally good full-time furrier may be the best place in town to get bargains on furs. Tremendous savings can be found on Geoffrey Beene, Basile Furs, and Shearlings. Financing is available. Coats normally selling for $14,000–$22,000 thousand can be found at Goldin Feldman for $4,000–$8,000 thousand. Park free at 241 West 28th Street. All sales are final. For mink sample sales, try **Mink Originals** at 145 West 30th Street, 9th Floor (736-4290). See chapter 11, "Outerwear."

HILTON MANUFACTURING COMPANY
35 East Elizabeth Avenue, Linden, New Jersey
201/486-2610
Checks with proper I.D.
Closed Sunday

This major supplier to retailers holds its own product sale several times a year, with merchandise priced much lower than it goes for in the stores. Hilton is a crowded warehouse, spacious and well-designed, and *the* place for men's and women's business suits, and women's skirts, dresses, and fine designer clothing. See chapter 12, "Menswear."

AIDA'S & JIM'S MERCHANDISING COMPANY
41 West 28th Street, 2nd Floor
689-2415
American Express, MC, Visa
Closed Saturday and Sunday
(open Saturdays in September)

Stock and samples of children's clothing are here at wholesale prices and below, in sizes infant to 14 years. They carry everything for the youngster, including pants, shirts, ensembles, even notebooks and other classroom items. Aida's opens Saturdays in September, when kids need clothes badly. See chapter 14, "Children's Wear." Also, every so often this sample mainstay has women's dresses, priced from $12–$60.

SUPERIOR OPTICAL COMPANY
1133 Broadway, Suite 223
677-6336
MC, Visa
Checks accepted

Here's an unusual bonus—sample sales in frames and non-designer (no color) contact lenses. Since 1940, this company has been dropping the prices on frames by Giorgio Armani, Robert La Roche, Laura Biagiotti, Missoni, Alfa Romeo, Polo, Safilo, Rodenstock, Sophia Loren, and Ray-Ban. You can even spot Porsche shades in this second-story glasses palace. Try-ons are certainly permitted. See chapter 5, "Shop-by-Mail."

CHAPTER 4

Flea Markets

This chapter is filled with places that you can't usually call; that have quixotic hours; that change their products almost weekly; that will for the most part accept only cash; and that are notoriously stubborn about their prices.

FURNITURE

The biggest New York City flea market for antiques is held during the last weekend of March at **Piers 88, 90, and 92** at the New York Passenger Ship Terminals. On the Sunday after Labor Day you will find the **TAMA County Fair** at Third Avenue between East 13th and 14th Streets, where small antiques line the avenue (entrances to sidestreets are closed to vehicles).

Other markets where furniture can be found include the **Annex Antiques Fair** at 26th Street and Sixth Avenue (Saturday and Sunday, 9 a.m.–5 p.m., $1 admission and worth it—see **Sixth Avenue Flea Market** below); the **Canal Street Flea Market** at Canal and Greene Street (weekends); the **Soho Canal Antique Market** at 369 Canal Street; and the **Roosevelt Raceway Flea Market,** at the former raceway out on Long Island (weekends; directions, 516/222-1530).

The following sales take place weekends: **P.S. 41 Flea Market,** located at Greenwich Avenue, between Sixth and Seventh Avenues. Call 751-4932. At this stop small *tschachkes* and large furniture pieces, even full-sized hutches, can be found. Furniture dealers and truckers with merchandise deriving from North Carolina sell leftover pieces here dirt cheap. Also, a small outlet called **Furniture Sales,** at 425 West 13th Street, stores old furniture pieces and pays cash for your leftovers. Lastly, at an outdoor mart at the corner of Seventh Avenue and Charles Street in the West Village, a woman named Josephine sells vintage furniture for a few hundred dollars. Josephine is not a full-time street saleslady; she is only there on Saturday. Still, she has numerous repeat customers.

See chapter 19, "Furniture."

OTHER FLEAS

Walter's World Famous Union Square Shoppes (873 Broadway, 255-0175; open Tuesday through Saturday, 10 a.m.–6 p.m.) has sixteen small shops that sell estate and costume jewelry and expensive artwork.

Battery Park Crafts Show, Bryant Park Crafts Show, and the **Yorkville Flea Market** all sell old china, unusual pottery, and some strange jewelry. But warning: shop at your own risk. At all three I have witnessed vendors making fools out of their customers by not listing prices and giving each person who approaches a completely different cost for items. (See the end of this chapter for tips on buying from sidewalk vendors.) But for an adventure, go to Battery Park (State Street, Bowling Green station and

Pearl Street, 752-8475) on Thursday only; the Bryant Park Show (42nd Street at Sixth Avenue) on Friday only; and Yorkville (351 East 74th Street, inside Jan Hus Presbyterian Church) on Saturday in summer.

Tower Market has nothing to do with Tower Records even though they are both located on Broadway between West Fourth and Great Jones Streets (for information, 718/273-8702). Here you will notice some of the most extraordinary T-shirt and sweatshirt collections, in addition to wool sweaters, fine and costume jewelry, fun hair ornaments, and other clothing accessories from Eastern Europe and Latin America! Tower Market is open Saturday and Sunday only. Remember to walk down Broadway to Houston Street, where "The Honest" sells fresh fruit at unbeatable (New York City) prices. For street vendors, see chapter 21, "Services and Unusual Bargains."

SIXTH AVENUE FLEA MARKET

As mentioned, a flea market is held on Saturday and Sunday, 9 a.m.–5 p.m., from West 24th to West 26th Streets along Sixth Avenue. It includes some two hundred vendors and a lot of good conversation. Dealers hawk used clothing, jewelry, and household items. (The **Annex Antiques Fair** cost $1, but the flea market is free.) Artists say this is *the* place to go for memorabilia such as postcards and photos from the old days, and unusual items like fabrics, baseball cards, old Coke bottles, and rhinestone earrings.

THE PUSHCART/JOBLOT
140 Church Street
962-4142
MC, Visa

This is not precisely a flea market, but look inside and you may be fooled: like a modern day general store, there's everything from small home appliances to black-boards, nail polish, typing paper, and diskettes for home computers, all at off-truck prices. Unlike other job lotters around town—imitations have sprung up everywhere, but this is the original—the clerks speak English, Spanish, and Yiddish. Everything sits in bins, because items are literally dropped off here by the truckload. This place buys the most unusual selection around of job lot merchandise (rough translation, "stuff that falls off trucks") and also acquires items from companies that have gone bankrupt, companies that need cash, United States Customs, and from other inexplicable sources.

As I mentioned previously, you will always do better shopping at places that buy merchandise in quantity. At Pushcart, where the slogan "A bargain is our business" is a reality, you will find surprising numbers of small gadgets, at a 50 percent reduction. (For more gadgets, try the **City Dump** at 332 Canal Street, 966-5651; open Sundays).

WBAI HOLIDAY CRAFTS FAIR
Fridays, Saturdays, and Sundays in December
695-4465

At only $6 per person admission, you can't go wrong here for Christmas gifts: a unique way to buy crafts *and* help a political cause. All proceeds benefit listener-supported radio station WBAI. You will find over 350 carefully selected craftspeople selling art to the public at this yearly extravaganza, from fiber-wearable art to crocheted or silk-screened goods. Also for sale are homemade toys and games—safe, sturdy ideas for kids—and a wide assortment of unusually designed home furnishings such as clocks, bureaus, mirrors, tapestries, quilts, pillows, and lamps. Also find collapsable wooden baskets, musical instruments, kaleidoscopes, candles, rugs, cocktail hats, and baby clothing! I highly recommend this place as a one-stop shopping mart.

POLICE AND POST OFFICE AUCTIONS

These are flea-like specials. The **Police Department Auctions** (4715 Pierson Place, Queens; information and dates, 212/406-1369) are held monthly at Pierson Warehouse. You can purchase small confiscated and lost items but you have to put up with a headache: You are required to view the merchandise a day beforehand. Then you have to purchase a small paddle ($20) to bid with. Then you riffle through a catalogue searching for items to match the bidding number. Then you bid.

At the frequent **Post Office Auctions** (General Post Office, 380 West 33rd Street; information and dates, 330-2932) you can obtain undeliverable mailed goods. To know precisely what items are being auctioned at the event, you again must attend a viewing beforehand. Take a brochure and mark it up well. Then listen carefully for the coveted item, as the auctioneer barely calls out the lot numbers. Since the GPO is auctioning center for the entire Northeast, you'll often see worthwhile merchandise.

MANHATTAN'S TWO MAIN AUCTION CENTERS

Sotheby's (1334 York Avenue, 606-7245) auctions prints, paintings, sculptures, fine furniture, and "decorations." Viewing hours are Monday through Saturday, 9 a.m.–5 p.m.; Sunday, 1–5 p.m. Before bidding day the viewings close at around 3 p.m. Cash, personal checks, and money orders are accepted.

Christie's (502 Park Avenue, 546-1000) is famous for rugs, glass and ceramics, contemporary art, and Impressionist prints. Viewings are a few days prior, catalogues cost $30.

Christie's East (219 East 67th Street, 606-0400) has less costly merchandise and puts catalogues out a month before bidding day. Experts say it's the perfect place for a first-timer. Only cash and personal checks are accepted.

CONNECTICUT'S GRAND SHOWS

Connecticut's flea markets include the **Antique/Craft Show at Holy Cross High School** in Waterbury (exit 18 off I-84; directions, 203/757-9248), which features over 100 exhibitors once a month. The **Jeff Jacobs Flea Market,** every Sunday in Plainville (exit 34 off I-84; directions, 203/242-1849), has collectibles, new furniture, and over 100 dealers at one indoor site. The **Old Mystic Flea Market** occurs a few days each month in the wonderful ancient town of Old Mystic (exit 90 off I-95; directions, 203/536-2223), with over 50 dealers. They sell small merchandise ranging from clothing to teddy bears. This, by the way, is a triple good time: shop at Old Mystic, see the famous Mystic Seaport in the next town, *and* get your pictures developed cheaply at **Mystic Color Labs!**

Lastly, **Wright's Barn Flea Market** is open every Saturday and Sunday in Torrington (exit 44 off I-84; directions, 203/482-0095), with thirty dealers and a host of assorted goods including lamps and dining room chair separates. Torrington is full of bed-and-breakfast stopovers if you desire a weekend away.

NOT-QUITE-FLEA-MARKETS

The **Little Red Schoolhouse** fair sells crafts by local artists on Sunday in the park attached to the school at the southeast corner of Bleecker Street and Sixth Avenue. There are some small furniture pieces, too.

Finally there's the **AACA Craftsfair,** sponsored in various upstate locations in the early spring and featuring miles of clothing and furniture bargains. This one is for super flea-goers. For bus and tour information call 413/787-0140.

HOW TO SHOP STREET VENDORS

Use these tips to deal with undependable street vendors, who have special ways of dealing with *street buyers:* Try to avoid buying appliances from sidewalk sellers, as many have learned the fine art of shrink-wrap. They might be selling you stolen or discarded merchandise that's been made to look new. Ralph Lauren Polo shirts sold on the street are counterfeit—you can tell because on the lapel, the designer's signature horse has only three legs! As for a popular street item known as the Cartier watch, according to Ralph Destion, chairman of Cartier, these devices are all counterfeit, and if you spot one, he would appreciate a call. He once took a law enforcement official on a short walk along Fifth Avenue; they came across hundreds of phony Cartiers being sold on the sidewalk. The chairman and the officer confiscated the watches and subsequently held a public watch crushing along Fifth. It was a neat event; the stretch of avenue was closed for an hour!

Lastly: Establish a maximum price. . . . Examine items carefully. . . . Don't be too anxious. . . . Never take a price quote seriously (haggle). . . . Let the sellers talk, for it usually makes them nervous and more willing to come down in price. . . . Pay cash and get an even greater discount. . . . Never negotiate too loudly—if you do you may get stuck with the same price offered to a nearby customer.

CHAPTER 5

Shop-by-Mail

FOTO CELL
49 West 23rd Street, 2nd Floor, New York, NY
924-7474
American Express, MC, Visa

Get in high gear with the best source for car stereos, alarms, radar detectors, and car gadgets. Choose from Uniden, Kenwood, Whistler, Cobra, Bel, Road Runner, Maxon and Fox detectors, and Kenwood, Denon, Jensen, Blaupunkt, and Sony stereos. This store has daily specials, advertised coupons, and a mail-order catalogue that few can beat. Everything is 7 to 17 percent above cost! See chapter 21, "Services and Unusual Bargains."

J & R MUSIC WORLD
Dept. 9003, 59-50 Queens-Midtown Expressway,
Maspeth, NY 11378
800/221-8180
American Express, MC, Visa, certified checks and
money orders

First, order the catalogue (800/426-6027) and then find special savings on amplifiers and highest quality stereo equipment, CDs, records, cassettes, videos, and computer software. Products carry manufacturer's warranties. Among the brands are Zenith, Packard, Panasonic, Casio, Technics, Pioneer, Sony, and Memorex. Every item is factory fresh—brand new—and fully guaranteed. See chapter 20, "Home Appliances."

PRO VIDEO DISTRIBUTORS
142-B Jericho Turnpike, Mineola, NY 11501
516/741-5440
MC, Visa

Find great deals on camcorders, video accessories, VCRs, and transfer equipment. Pro Video carries Canon, Panasonic, Sony, Minolta, Olympus, Ricoh, Toshiba, JVC, Zenith, Hitachi, and much more. All their pricetags include warranties, factory-sealed boxes, and a ten-day money-back guarantee. They gladly ship anywhere. You can call their price quote line toll-free at 800/541-4055. See chapter 20, "Home Appliances."

WALDENVIDEO BY MAIL
Dept. 643, P.O. Box 4990, Stamford, CT 06907
800/443-7359
American Express, MC, Visa, checks, money orders

Video collectors get an opportunity to supplement their libraries with a little help from the Waldenbooks firm. Great gift items are featured in a catalogue of videos to suit every taste. Comedy classics, children's stories, bestsellers, musicals, foreign films, cult movies, action/ adventure, and new releases are all fully guaranteed. Orders are shipped in one or two days. See chapter 17, "Stationery and Household Items."

EURO-TIRE
567 Route 46, P.O. Box 1198-C, Fairfield, NJ 07004
201/575-0080
American Express, MC, Visa

At Euro-Tire you can choose from an enormous selection of tires, wheels, and shock absorbers. Their entire stock is strictly first quality and is warranteed against normal use and defects in materials and workmanship with no time or mileage limitations. Featured brands include Continental, Pirelli, Kleber, and Yokohama. See Chapter 22, "Novelties and Gift Items."

DIAL-A-MATTRESS
800/999-1000
American Express, MC, Visa

A must if you live in the tri-state area: simply dial MATTRES, and, as their slogan says, "Leave off the last 'S' for savings!" Shop the stores for the model numbers of Sealy Posturpedic, Serta Perfect Sleeper, and Simmons Beauty Rest—then call this number for best prices. Note: open 6 a.m. to midnight all year round. For a small fee, you can have your mattress delivered the same day. See chapter 17, "Stationery and Household Items."

ELDRIDGE TEXTILE COMPANY
277 Grand Street, New York, NY 10002
925-1523
MC, Visa, checks, money orders

Sheets, pillow cases, comforters, and towels with such

brand names as Laura Ashley, Martex, Wamsutta, Stevens, Utica, and Fieldcrest are sold at tremendous savings through Eldridge. In addition to their extensive line of bed linens and towels, they carry a full array of bedspreads, comforter sets, curtains, blankets, quilts, and shower curtains (all bathroom accessories can be found here, too). Call for free catalogue. Orders are shipped UPS if stocked. See chapter 17, "Stationery and Household Items."

HARRIS LEVY IMPORTERS
278 Grand Street, New York, NY 10002
226-3102 ✓
American Express, MC, Visa

Harris Levy features an array of close to one hundred styles and patterns of sheets from every mill, such as Wamsutta, Martex, and JP Stevens. Virtually every designer is represented, including top quality in towels, like Fieldcrest and Martex. They also have a large selection of kitchen items, bath accessories, and table linens. See chapter 17, "Stationery and Household Items."

WAMSUTTA FACTORY OUTLETS
1340 Tunnel Road, Asheville, NC 28805
~~**704/298-3393**~~
MC, Visa

No shop-by-mail list could be complete without a note about the finest quality bed linens, comforters, flannel sheet sets, towels, and bathroom accessories from current and past seasons, all from the collections of Christian Dior and Wamsutta. They have two locations in South Carolina and one in Georgia, and all you need for great savings is to call with the pattern name. Savings are 20 percent off retail. Incidentally, Wamsutta is glad to serve directly the customers who normally buy their goods in stores. See chapter 17, "Stationery and Household Items."

B DISCOUNT MARINE
Meadow Road, Edison, NJ 08817
800/533-5007
American Express, MC, Visa

Buy marine accessories at discount prices from E & B's enormous selection, "where America buys its boating supplies." Call or write for free 136-page catalogue and receive fast, friendly, and knowledgeable service. Merchandise is shipped by UPS, parcel post or Federal Express within 48 hours. See chapter 22, "Novelties and Gift Items."

MATERNITY WAREHOUSE OUTLET
2402 Maple Avenue, Burlington, NC 27215
800/USA-MOMS
American Express, MC, Visa, checks, money orders

Here you can order anything you might need to be an attractive expectant mother. They have apparel for casual, career, and evening wear—and postpartum outfits, too. To top it off, they have a line of lingerie and nursing clothes and equipment. Exchanges are accepted. See chapter 13, "Womenswear."

NO NONSENSE BRAND NAMES (FOR LESS)
2515 East 43rd Street, Chattanooga, TN 37407
~~615/867-1302~~
MC, Visa, checks, money orders

This catalogue has No Nonsense panty hose and Bestform girdles and bras on sale at extraordinary prices. Underwear, bras, socks, girdles, and more can be had at big savings in the brands Playtex, Burlington, and First Quality, as well as No Nonsense. This is a jam-packed catalogue. See chapter 13, "Womenswear."

CURRENT, INC.
1025 E. Woodmen Rd.
Colorado Springs, CO 80918
719/593-5900
MC, Visa

There are tremendous savings to be found here on greeting cards, paper goods, handy computer supplies, gift wrap, and other things you'd find at your local Hallmark shop. Also, free shipping and quantity discounts are offered. Send $1 for a catalogue. See chapter 17, "Stationery and Household Items."

TOTES FACTORY OUTLET
3163 Outlet Boulevard, Myrtle Beach, SC 29577
803/236-6389
MC, Visa

Closeouts of luggage, scarves, raincoats, hats and rubbers, in addition to everything in the Totes label. This outlet store carries overstocks and some irregulars in Totes and associated brands. Shop at a retail store and then call the factory outlet to see how much. Merchandise is shipped in ten days. See chapter 11, "Outerwear."

BLOOMINGDALE'S BY MAIL
475 Knotter Drive, Cheshire, CT 06410
203/271-1313
American Express, MC, Visa, checks, money orders

Bloomie's comes into your home via a gigantic catalogue. All the fashion and products you've come to expect from the store—well, almost anything. The bakery's raspberry mousse can't be shipped! This eclectic catalogue includes housewares, linens, and some "unusual accessories" for women, as well as clothing in every size, color, and style, shipped (usually) in three days. See chapter 13, "Womenswear."

BOOT TOWN WAREHOUSE OUTLET
2821 LBJ Freeway, Farmer's Branch, TX 75234
214/243-1151
American Express, MC, Visa

This outlet offers up to 85 percent off on men's and ladies' boots including Laredo Ropers and Panhandle Slim, plus a wide selection of cowboy paraphernalia. Hats are here, of course. You can return the boots if you decide they aren't right for you. For more shoes by mail, see **Dunham** and **Minnetonka** in chapter 1, "Shoes!" and for more shoe news, see chapter 4, "Flea Markets."

UNITED PHARMACAL CO. (UPCO)
P.O. Box 969, St. Joseph, MO 64502
816/233-8809
American Express, MC, Visa, checks, money orders, C.O.D.s

Pet supplies are the specialty here, for dogs, horses, and felines, with new merchandise offered through seasonal catalogues. They can ship you antibiotics, wormers, instruments, vitamins, insecticides, grooming aids, feeders, books, and skin treatments. And of course the ordinary accessories are available, too, such as flea collars, leashes, toys, books, and coat brushes. If you combine your orders with friends you can qualify for quantity prices. See chapter 21, "Services and Unusual Bargains."

DIAL A CONTACT LENS
470 Nautilus Street, Suite 209, La Jolla, CA 92037
800/238-LENS
American Express, MC, Visa, checks, money orders

An innovation of our ever-quickening society: call with a prescription and a credit card number, and lenses are whisked to you in days. The brands include Bausch & Lomb, Barnes-Hind Hydrocurve, Wesley Jessen, CIBA, and Suntex. No color lenses available, though. Delivery is by mail, and any defects must be reported within three days. See chapter 22, "Novelties and Gift Items."

VICTORIA'S SECRET OF LONDON
P.O. Box 16589, Columbus, OH 43216
800/888-8200
American Express, MC, Visa, checks, money orders

One of the best-known names in lingerie and fancy nightgowns (with a dozen different teddies) will send you a spread of clothing selections designed to titillate. Their catalogue includes pages of wild designer nighties. There is also upscale clothing for women. You can always get a refund if you are not satisfied with the effects of your purchase! See chapter 13, "Womenswear," and chapter 22, "Novelties and Gift Items."

BURLINGTON BAG & BAGGAGE
Highway 62, Burlington, NC 27215
919/226-7352
MC, Visa, checks, money orders

Up to 30 percent savings on over three hundred makes of better handbags, luggage, ladies' shoes, and accessories. Go to a local store and jot down the SKU number, then phone up Burlington. The types you will find here include Lark, Samsonite, London Fog, and many more. See Chapter 18, "Luggage and Carry-Alls."

CHAPTER 6

New Jersey

SECAUCUS

Woe to the shopping expert who doesn't know Secaucus. Three complexes feature many outlets located in one spot:

For Castle Road Outlet Center, take Route 3 East (exit 16 W) to Meadowland Parkway until you reach Castle Road. There you will feast your eyes on some twenty thousand square feet of factory stores and distributor outlet stores, offering savings ranging from 20 to 80 percent, depending on the store. There is a great deal of parking and, while the city's Port Authority (564-8484) offers bus service to and from, you might want to rent a car to get from complex to complex.

At Castle Road: **Adidas** offers 25 to 70 percent savings on footwear, shirts, and other actionwear. The **Giftwarehouse Outlet** sells Capidamonte pieces that can save you 35 percent off regular prices. **Tops 'N Bottoms** sells designer sportswear—Geoffrey Beene, Yves St. Laurent, and Liz Claiborne—with savings of up to 50 percent. **VIP Mill Stores** is the craft supply shop that houses Wintuk, Sayelle, and Dazselaire yarns at a savings of 30 to 60 percent on stitchery knits. Also, you can find needlework including crewel, needlepoint, and cross-stitch. **Apparel Connection** has up to 80 percent savings on pants, skirts, blouses, sweaters, and more. **Calvin Klein Outlet Store** is a full service center with regular closeouts on designer sportswear for men and casual sportswear for women. **Church's English Shoe Shop** is a fine place for men to find a dependable leather shoe for 50 percent off—all by Church and Clark. **Danson Jewelers** has a 20 percent savings on stones and diamonds. Also, they do very inexpensive repairs. **Diamond Masquerade** has accessories and a large range of Swiss watches at 30 percent off the Swiss manufacturer's regular price. The **Kidstuff Factory Outlet** is accessories and regular apparel (from Gap to imported stock) at a slight discount. **L'Eggs, Hanes and Bali Factory Outlet** offers a discount up to 50 percent off retail prices on L'eggs, Hanes, Bali, and Gem Dandy hosiery, lingerie, socks, and sweatsuits. They have a Hosiery Club membership that can earn you six free pairs after you purchase seventy-two pairs of the same. **Marburn Curtain Warehouse** can save you a bundle on curtains, linens, and rugs. **Mighty Mac Factory Direct Store** offers a 50 percent retail discount on toddler, infant, and adolescent clothing and outerwear—including rainwear and overcoats. **Toy Liquidators** is almost a carbon copy of Manhattan's Kiddie City center, with about 50 percent savings on toys from Mattel, Fisher-Price, Kenner, Ideal, Tonka, Playskool, Tomy, Matchbox, Coleco, Milton Bradley, Tyco, Hasbro, and, believe it or not, more. Lastly, **Sportswear Systems** is a designer sportswear outlet with Fenn Wright & Manson clothing for women. Skirts, blouses, blazers, and slacks are all sold at about 50 percent off. This is one of the few places women can get this designer's products at such a discount. The store is beautiful.

Harmon Cove Outlet Center is right by Castle Road. It has thirty factory outlets and a food court for light meals and coffee. Not all the stores are quite factory outlets, but you will find discounts everywhere.

What's inside Harmon Cove: **Accessories Plus** and **Plus II Athlete's Outlet** with Pony footwear and other items at 40 percent off. Both men's and women's sport shoes are featured. **Bally** has elegant briefcases and matched goods with a savings of 60 percent. Bally shoes are also featured, as are handbags (also at 60 percent off). **Barbizon Lingerie** is featured in other factory centers throughout the country: a 40 percent savings on pajamas, slips, half-slips, camisoles, and short and long robes. Not only the Barbizon brand but also Hanes, Dearfoam, and Angeltreads. **Bass Shoe Factory Outlet** store has a 50 percent discount on suggested retail prices for women's shoes, selling Weejuns, Bucs, Sunjuns, and others. The **Children's Outlet** offers savings of 10 percent on retail prices of boys' and girls' clothing, sizes newborn to 14. **Designer Luggage Depot** has up to 75 percent off Samsonite, Oscar de la Renta, Gloria Vanderbilt, and John Weitz brands. Try **Executive Neckwear** for 30 percent off wallets, ties, and gift items for women and men. Brands include Pierre Cardin, Buxton, Prince Gardner, John Henry, Swank, Johnny Carson, Halston, and Alexander Julian. All leather goods are 50 percent off on special sale days. **Fashion Flair** is part of a chain that carries the Izod brand (Lacoste's "alligator" shirts) at a 40 percent discount, and carries Monet for men and children. **Gitano Factory Store** is a famous outlet with up to 50 percent off women's and girls' dresses, accessories, footwear, outerwear, underwear, and pocket T-shirts. It also has a good selection of maternity clothes. **Intimate Eve,** formerly St. Eve, has unique lingerie selections at savings of almost 50 percent. They also have pajamas in stock. **Van Heusen Factory Outlet,** carrying a leader in men's fashion, has 50 percent off Van Heusen shirts, in addition to a fine line of accessories, sweaters, outerwear, and a collection of women's sweaters. **Perfume Plus** is certainly a plus, for in this location you will find a 70 percent savings on fragrances and cosmetics from Nina Ricci, Almay, Revlon, Polo, Fendi, Liz Claiborne, and Max Factor. Also remaining at Harmon Cove is the **Tahari** retailer with 50 percent off dresses, suits, and blouses for women. Lastly, the **WilliWear** outlet carries a smattering of the famous designer Willie Smith's clothing for men and women—at about 40 percent off retail price.

And there's a bonus: Enterprise Avenue, the third center in Secaucus, has **United Status Apparel,** a warehouse that features moderately priced sportswear from Carole Little and Adrienne Vittadini. Sometimes they will go as high as 70 percent off on first quality designer women's apparel. Plus, **Calvin Klein** has another shop on Enterprise. There's the **China, Glass, and Gift Outlet** at 25 Enterprise. The well-known manufacturer **Mikasa** keeps a service center here with their stock marked down 50 percent. You might visit their New York City showroom first, at 28 West 23rd Street, then go to Secaucus. Finally, **Wholesaler's Shoe Outlet** is just off Enterprise Avenue. See chapter 1, "Shoes!"

Note: At all three complexes, major credit cards are accepted and stores are open seven days a week. Keep in mind that on Sunday all stores are open from 12–5 p.m. For information and a packet describing how to get around Secaucus's many factory centers, write to Outlet Center, P.O. Box 2187, Secaucus, NJ 07096.

BURLINGTON

Burlington is unpretentious. Just take a walk or drive through this old country town in the area Jerseyites call "609 territory" (area code for southern New Jersey) and you'll notice small-town all-purpose candy stores and tributes to war dead on the main streets. Willingboro Mall on Route 130 is located near the small furniture (**Bucci**) and carpet outlets (**Forcellini**), both advertising "art" and coming through. There is a good amount of style at a fraction of the price—all of it along the main drag in this small town.

For example—and there are plenty in Burlington—there are the **Burlington Coat Factory** and the recently opened **Capezio Shoe Outlet** with every imaginable style and size.

The Coat Factory in itself is a spectacle. Inside are 20–70 percent savings on men's and women's outerwear, linens, clothes for all ages, an incredible baby toy and *tschachke* department, and an impressive selection of kids' accessories and newfangled toys. In fact, Burlington Coat Factory houses objects ranging from full-length furs to kitchen utensils (all this year's models). Nowhere else can you find such a selection of women's and girls' hats. It's a department store with several factory outlets under one roof! In addition, clearance sales of new items are fantastic, even though Burlington is still an old-fashioned hometown store.

After the Coat Factory, go to the various side streets off Route 130: High Street has bargains both west and east of the highway. West you'll see pet and costume shops, east the famed soap and linen hangout **All-in-One,** a supermarket of 40 percent savings on towels, bedding, and percales. From the outside you expect to be besieged by cardboard boxes of merchandise; indoors you encounter nicely-scented rooms filled with bed and bath notions. It's a gift buyer's paradise and, come December, madness breaks loose at All-in-One.

Then there are the two Salem Street mini-marts, on Salem, off 130. One is the odd-looking **Burlington Mart,** east of the highway, which houses an **Annie Sez** outlet, several funny junk shops, and a **Ship 'n Shore** for women's blouses, shirts, knits, and sportswear. The other is the **Village Fashion Outlet,** which mostly sells misses and juniors dresses.

But wait, there's more. Heading back on 130, stop in at **G & J Art Pieces** for fine paintings at prices below wholesale. They will bargain with any "decent offer."

Call Burlington Coat Factory's knowledgeable local staff at 609/386-3314 and they will gladly give you more information on this town, a shopper's haven.

FLEMINGTON

Flemington's Liberty Village has so many places to shop in one town. The **Dansk Factory Outlet** has the largest collection of china, cookware, and giftware, displayed so stylishly that you find yourself enchanted and more willing than ever to purchase things you didn't realize you needed! Everything is 20 percent off, and when overstocked they drop it an additional 10 percent. Most shopping towns are rather ambivalent about their visitors. Not so at Flemington, where everyone greets you like a long-lost friend.

The Flemington Traffic Circle is right in the middle of it all, with the Flemington Outlet Center nearby: find there **Samples Women's Collection** of juniors and misses closeouts; **Village Outlet** for women's clothes, with surprises shipped daily in all sizes; the **Kitchen Place** for utensils and tools for the most-used room in the house; and **Windsor Shirt Company** for men.

Then there's Liberty Village and Turntable Junction on Church Street in Flemington with eighty shops and restaurants in a village setup. This isn't colonial Williamsburg, so don't expect prices from out of the past, but the number of distributors and collections here make it a worthwhile stopover for shopping enthusiasts.

It includes the **Anne Klein Outlet,** where you will find Anne's outfits and Dona Karan, too; **Joan & David,** the shoe store outlet; and the **Calvin Klein** shop. Here you can see Calvin's best goods at 20 percent off store prices. (Many of the items are last year's clothing, but they're not outmoded.) Another good bet is the **Royal Doulton** shop, with some 50 percent savings on dinnerware, giftware, and crystal. Here you will also see seconds and closeouts of such names as Royal Albert, Tony, and Beatrix Potter.

Bagmakers Factory Store features fine luggage and handbags at 25 percent off; the **Beauty Scenter** sells fine perfumes and bath oils at 40 percent off; **Corning Ware** factory outlet offers a 50 percent discount on every item, including a fine selection of Corning patterns.

Also see the crystal collection at **Kosta Boda,** replete with crystal, china, and assorted items well suited for gifts. For kids, **Doe-Spun** can grant you clothing values, including for newborns. Savings can be as high as 70 percent (they start at 20 percent and go up as the item sits around). **Hamilton Factory** sells clocks; some samples or floor models are sold for 80 percent off retail price.

Call 201/782-8550 for more on Flemington, New Jersey's only small town devoted to you, the shopper.

CHAPTER 7

Best of
Orchard Street

MITCHELL
33 Orchard Street
925-6757
MC, Visa
Closed Saturday

You might never expect to find such a delightful leathergoods store on Orchard Street. Here are men's, women's, even teen's jackets and coats of fine quality, even full-length coats, fur linings, and the finer lamb leather. You'll get an automatic 20 percent discount from retail prices, in addition to 30 to 40 percent off selected coats at all times. Alterations are inexpensive. See chapter 11, "Outerwear."

FRIEDLICH INC.
196 Orchard Street
254-8899
American Express, MC, Visa

Here you'll see every kind of coat imaginable, at savings of up to 70 percent, and often major sales that only get advertised in the windows! This is an old-style shop that has all the top French designers, and even Calvin Klein, on hand. The basement is where they keep the discounted top designers' coats—"the finer cut," they advertise. Upstairs on the main floor you'll find the less expensive racks with mostly domestic brands. In addition to coats, the store stocks skirts and other fine fashions. See chapter 11, "Outerwear."

EUROPA
163 Orchard Street
477-1083
American Express, MC, Visa

Leather and fur-lined coats and hats are well arrayed at Europa. They pride themselves on bringing in good outerwear from the manufacturers *before* the major retailers get their stock. Here you see moderate discounts of 20 percent off retail prices on purchases above $200, 10 to 15 percent when the merchandise is less. In business for six years, Europa expands the store and stock yearly. Some 90 percent of their stock is from European manufacturers, hence the name. See chapter 11, "Outerwear."

TREVI
141 Orchard Street
505-0293
American Express, MC, Visa

Women's, children's, and some men's shoes are sold at 1/3 off store prices. Trevi gets only the "avant-garde" designers from Europe, mostly Italian, and sells the same brands that Madison Avenue hawks, only at 20 to 40 percent less. These include Claudia Lucci, Jean-Marco Lorenzi, and Lonzoni Lan. Trevi believes in the latest model, and stocks it well. The store is designed not to be a crowded outlet, but a fashionable discount shoe mall. There are some companies that are domestic in origin, too, such as Vivaldi and Baldino. They recently expanded their stock of children's shoes, taking over the store next door. There you will find yourself staring at the same brands that the now defunct Boticellini shop in Trump Tower sold. They also have an odd selection of purses. Everything is discounted directly on the tag. See chapter 1, "Shoes!"

TOBALDINI
140 Orchard Street
477-0507
American Express, MC, Visa
Closed Saturday

At Tobaldini, see children's clothes—including stock for newborns—all imported from Europe and the Far East. They have Gianni Versace, Moscino, Trotinette, and Vlimax. Everything is about 25 percent off retail prices, but sometimes the manager adds merchandise to a rack and finds he has to raise the discount to 40 percent, to alleviate stock overload. Newborn and infant merchandise includes toddler sizes from 10 months up. Ask about in-store monthly closeouts. See chapter 14, "Children's Wear."

FINE & KLEIN
119 Orchard Street
674-6720
Check or money order
Closed Saturday

This has been a browser's paradise for 45 years. All types of women's designer clothes, including some of the bigger names, are here. You will find a lot of Bob Mackie, too, and hats—a third off whatever you'd find uptown.

Sometimes the women's department will have automatic closeouts of up to 75 percent on a certain designer. They have a second building next door, that includes an accessories department; a well-stocked shoe section housing Nippon, Sony, Ferro; and handbags, thousands of handbags neatly piled in the back of their second store. Discounts for them run up to 50 percent. See chapter 13, "Womenswear."

BECKENSTEIN FABRICS
130 and 135 Orchard Street
529-8211
American Express, MC, Visa
Closed Saturday

Two stores are now at Beckenstein: one is the Home Fabric Store, and the other is Beckenstein's Ladies Fabric. The former will help you get your house in order with upholstery, custom measuring and installation of wallpaper, and all drapery hardware. They cut the cotton prints down to $2 a yard and in most cases you can even have a window treatment or a bedspread ordered out of their catalogue. You can either order the material or have them make it for you. As for women's clothing, they have the stock for sewing buffs that has made Beckenstein's a household name for dressmakers since early in this century. A three thousand square feet addition means they can now help you put together a new couch by purchasing both the fabric and the couch direct from the manufacturer. As for fancy items like window treatments, you can buy festoons and jabots and give your living room a baroque look. See chapter 21, "Services and Unusual Bargains."

LACE-UP SHOES
110 Orchard Street
475-8040
American Express, MC, Visa
Closed Saturday

An old shoe store that keeps getting better, Lace-Up

has now hired some uptown sales clerks and turned their store from a crowded mess to a ladies' shoe paradise. In stock are Joan & David, Donna Karan, Yves St. Laurent, Anne Klein, Bandolino, and others. In addition to their regular 25 to 30 percent discounts, when the store is very busy they often give an automatic discount on a particular designer's whole stock—on a whim. This "fast-tracking" drops an entire selection of fine designer shoes to $40–$70. This is a good reason to go regularly to Lace-Up. They call it a "feeding frenzy." See chapter 1, "Shoes!"

FORMAN'S
82 Orchard Street
228-2500
Closed Friday at 4 p.m., all day Saturday
MC, Visa

I always figured Forman's, with four-plus clothing stores, owns Orchard Street. Every item in the main Forman's shop, the **Designer Apparel Mart** at #82 Orchard—others are at #94 (**Petite**) and #78 (**Plus**),—is a fine designer label, even though the low-priced stickers may be a little hard to discern. The Plus and Petite stores are good opportunities for those who have trouble finding clothes in the right size. The Designer Apparel Mart is a fine stop for misses and juniors, with 20 percent off everyday prices and a knowledgeable sales staff. Ask about their special sales, or look carefully at the sale racks in this main store, offering immediate markdowns. See chapter 13, "Womenswear."

GOLDMAN AND COHEN
55 Orchard Street
966-0737

This is a bra and girdle place for those looking to stock up. They carry robes and nightgowns, too. See chapter 13, "Womenswear."

LUGGAGE PLUS
83 Orchard Street
966-9744
American Express, MC
Closed Friday at 3 p.m., all day Saturday

Brands carried include Samsonite, Lark, American Tourister, Lucas, and Totes. The "Plus" in the store name covers specialty items such as attaché cases, umbrellas, and a wide selection of pens. Everything is 25–40 percent off retail, but can run as high as 50 percent when the manufacturers run special promotions. All luggage is featured as matched sets but they are always willing to separate. See chapter 18, "Luggage and Carry-Alls."

D & A MERCHANDISE
22 Orchard Street
925-4766
American Express, MC, Visa
Closed Saturday

The self-proclaimed "underwear king" (and queen, for it's a husband-and-wife operation) sells all types of undergarments—for men, jockeys, BVDs, and athletic supporters; for women, girdles, bras, and nighties. D & A is a nice spot for a gift of a fancy T-shirt with a wonderful, colorful saying. They feature a savings of 20 to 50 percent off prices at stores and gift marts. (It's *the* place for souvenirs.) See the inexpensive pajamas, eveningwear, and colorful longjohns, or take a gander at the men's nightshirt collection. See chapter 13, "Womenswear."

CHAPTER 8

Brooklyn
the Eclectic

ANTIQUES AT DALE'S
683 Coney Island Avenue
Kensington, Brooklyn, take "D/Q" to
Courtelyou Road
718/941-7059
Closed Tuesday

For six years this mix of predominantly twenties and thirties antique furniture has been building a clientele based on eclectic choices. The strengths here are lamps, bedroom sets, and furniture from entire estates. Their china cabinets are truly extraordinary, particularly when you see that the 2400 square feet store doesn't have that much room, and owner Walter Dale has to be choosy about what he allows in stock.

Prices are as low as possible, but Dale tries to get people to look at their purchases as "investments." This means you can buy something reasonable—say, a bedroom set for $200—and if it needs curved glass, you get *it* for an additional $250. If you have the furniture for a few years, it'll be worth thousands. See chapter 19, "Furniture."

TIME TRADER
368 Atlantic and stores across the street
Boerum Hill, Brooklyn, take "2/3/4/5" to
Nevins Street
718/352-3301
Checks accepted

You can't go wrong shopping here for antiques. It's a second-hand furniture store that stocks, in three nearby stores, pine, walnut, mahogany, and oak furniture of English, Scandinavian, and French origin (some American thrown in). The main store at #368 has three levels; it's where you come to look at the latest models. The warehouse store at 443 Atlantic is where you see specialty items.

They have recently added a full-service workshop for period reproduction work. And that, believe it or not, consists of reasonable, reliable custom work from samples that are right in the shop. This workshop is so successful that several Manhattan restaurants have used their services. Consumers find that by having someone design their furniture it becomes an economical way to get precisely what's wanted. Since they get monthly shipments from various suppliers, Trader is a must for the furniture aficionado. See chapter 19, "Furniture."

FABRIC ALTERNATIVE
78 Seventh Avenue
Park Slope, Brooklyn, take "2/3/4" to
Grand Army Plaza
718/857-5482
American Express, MC, Visa

At first this was a crafts store that sold fashion fabrics

and sewing supplies. But as with most good things, the rent went up and Fabric Alternative became a home decorating center—and one of the cheapest in the five boroughs. They employ a team of sewing people to work out of the shop; they will make you anything you want for your home, at about 40 percent less than the retail home decorating centers.

Fabric Alternative houses the largest collection of calicos around as well as a gigantic collection of specially designed children's fabrics. Custom sewing can be very inexpensive—you can get a sewing panel for as little as $12. A lavish damask that would go for $100 elsewhere sells here for $15! There are moirés, cottons, and chintzes—for window treatments, unusual slipcover designs, and nursery ensembles. Actually there isn't anything for the home that Fabric Alternative *can't* do for you. The store is only 600 square feet, so they work mostly by the book: books of fabrics and patterns, including an unusual collection of muted pastels and "wake-up" fabrics. Samples can be sent through the mail. See chapter 14, "Children's Wear."

NATIONAL COUNCIL THRIFT MART
255 Flatbush Avenue
Prospect Heights, Brooklyn, take "2/3/4" to
Bergen Street
718/622-2422
Closed Sunday

You won't believe the selection, courtesy of Brooklyn residents who donate to the National Council of Jewish Women. Men's and ladies' clothing, shoes, hats, bags, crystal, and jewelry—even a separate furniture store next door. The members of the council, many in number, give big, and donors themselves decide how much their "gift" will sell for. It makes for an unusual pricing structure.

Find Persian coats here and full shelves of brassware for sale, cheap. Most people come mainly to browse in the main store, which features knickknacks and bric-a-brac. However, the furniture store takes pride in the number of appliances they stock—televisions and large-scale radios—and there are entire living room sets available on most days. The large wicker hampers and typewriters in this separate space will surprise even jaded shoppers. See chapter 20, "Home Appliances."

VALUE HOSIERY
272 Fifth Avenue
Park Slope, Brooklyn, take "N/R" to Union Street
718/499-6721
American Express, MC, Visa
Closed Saturday and three hours before sundown on Friday

The Park Slope branch of Value Hosiery—which sells socks in several sections of Brooklyn—is one place all women can agree on: the best deal in Brooklyn on all kinds of socks for women *and* men, leotards, bathing suits and swimming paraphernalia, dancewear, shoes, pantyhose, and nylons. This store serves the corporate community, supplying fine and discount stores in the metropolitan area. But you can get it cheaper here.

When you walk through this big warehouse of a store, you will notice people checking out each bin for extra-special price tags. This is because Value Hosiery has an odd habit of pricing identical items differently—just to keep things interesting, I suppose. The owner, Larry Gavinda, says he has a "specific markup" in mind for everything. "Whatever price I buy it at, the markup remains the same," he told me. Which is why sometimes, as in their fine selection of dance shoes, prices can be extremely low. (They are often even less than the closeouts at danceclothier Capezio.) See chapter 13, "Womenswear."

FRANKEL'S DISCOUNT STORE
3924 Third Avenue
Sunset Park, Brooklyn, take "R" to 36th Street
718/768-9788
American Express, MC, Visa
Closed Sunday in summer only

For discounts on Western wear, people say, "Go into Brooklyn," where Frankel's has been making waves for years by selling Western boots for about 40 percent less than most.

The boots are their specialty item, featuring Timberland, Rockport, Frye, and Dan Post priced from $30 to $200. When there's a sale, you can get up to 80 percent off the older models. Boots make up about a third of the merchandise—the rest consists of discontinued cowboy shirts, gloves, down and leather jackets, and sneakers that usually sell for 80 percent more elsewhere. You can find exotic jeans, designer and unusual footwear (Reebok and Adidas, neon solids, tie-dyed sneakers), always at a discount. How much of a discount depends on the model year. If it's the latest sneaker, it'll be between 20 and 25 percent; if it's from last season, you can bet it'll be in the region of 80 percent off. Ski glasses, sweats, baseball cards, and whatever job-lot special the truck unloaded that week—all may show up at Brooklyn's own Frankel's! See chapter 1, "Shoes!"

V. J. JONES
138 DeKalb Avenue
Fort Greene, Brooklyn, take "B/D/M/N/Q/R" to
DeKalb Avenue
718/237-2613
American Express, MC, Visa

V. J. is a one-of-a-kind womenswear shop that sells

accessories, tummy tops, one-shoulder tops, pantsuits, coat dresses, and other exotic goods at a good price. Eric Javits hats, pricey and inexpensive, start at $47, and neckware by Ambiance starts at $35. Lines such as Opera, Vaux Pop, and FBI dot this store. The rest of the stock is lingerie ($5–$50), silk scarves (around $20), hot socks ($2–$10), and blazer dresses ($140–$160). See chapter 13, "Womenswear."

UNDERWORLD PLAZA
141 62nd Street
Borough Park, Brooklyn, take "B/M" to 62nd Street
718/232-6804, 837-2800
American Express, MC, Visa

Underworld Plaza is hot stuff—an outlet that sells camisoles, teddies, baby dolls, girdles, garter belts, slips, bathing suits, and panties: everything in intimate apparel. This monstrous bargain site is run by a major manufacturer of intimate wear who would be chagrined if too many people knew that the things they make for Marshall's, Lamston's, Alexander's, and Filene's Basement can be gotten for half-price at the Underworld outlet. Bill Blass, Christian Dior, and Bali Bras likewise do not volunteer the information that you can get their intimate apparel at Underworld instead of Bloomingdale's.

There are seasonal closeouts here—get on their mailing list or call them every so often. All winter robes are sold for around $25 at the end of the winter, and all swimwear is priced down at the end of summer. While the K-Marts and Woolworths of the world get the name brands distributed at a high markup—Calvin Klein boxer shorts and the newfangled 1930s bras—you can take advantage of Underworld's fantastic prices in Borough Park. Try-ons are fine; returns are, too. See chapter 13, "Womenswear."

CENTURY 21
472 86th Street
Bay Ridge, Brooklyn, take "R" to 86th Street
718/748-3266
American Express, MC, Visa, checks

I once read a book that said that New York had "thousands of treasures" for shoppers. When I noticed the book didn't mention Century 21, I put it down. Office know-it-alls will tell you without shame that you shouldn't go anywhere but here to stock up on women's clothing and shoes, men's clothing and outerwear, cosmetics, bathroom goodies, even Walkmans and linen. They have bins of designer outfits, bushels of skirts, racks of designer jeans, baby clothes, robes, sports clothing, and lingerie. The prices are below reasonable—sometimes 50 percent less than retail. One drawback: no try-ons are permitted. But the liberal return policy makes up for the difficulty. After all, once you discover Century you'll be back soon.

One of the nicest things about the Bay Ridge Century 21 is that it's open at 7:45 a.m. every weekday. The well-stocked but nowhere near as chock-filled **Manhattan branch of Century 21** is located at 12 Cortlandt Street (227-9092).

ALL IRELAND IRISH IMPORT STORE
8513 Third Avenue
Bay Bridge, Brooklyn, take "R" to 86th Street
718/748-9240
Checks accepted
Closed Sunday afternoon

This last store is truly unusual: everything for the lads and the lasses, all with an Irish brogue. Owner Pete Tuohy imports his sweaters direct from the Irish farms, and has a full line of Irish delicacies, including candies, blood pudding, and an assortment of fine meats (even infamous Irish bacon). The store is tiny, but there aren't many places you can find sweet Irish jewelry—including a bountiful collection of Claddagh rings and pins—hand-knit tams, scarves, and Ireland's own spectacular line of Waterford crystal.

When you need an excuse to go into a neighborhood, find an inexpensive one. Tuohy swears by a pricing motto: that every item he sells is just 30 percent above his cost. For imports, this is a good deal. See chapter 21, "Services and Unusual Bargains."

CHAPTER 9

Downtown Brooklyn and Flatbush

ABRAHAM & STRAUS
420 Fulton Street at the Fulton Mall
Downtown Brooklyn, take "A/C/G" to
Hoyt-Schermerhorn Streets
718/875-7200
American Express, MC, Visa

It's been almost 130 years since Abraham & Straus opened shop and became Brooklyn's first homegrown department store. And now they're everywhere, including Paramus, New Jersey and in a spanking new complex in downtown Manhattan. This one, the oldest A & S, is one of the nicest, most charming and old-fashioned shopping malls in the tri-state area. In one large but not boastful store, you will see a bargain basement, a toy department

overflowing with gift ideas, a beauty salon, a jewelry repair center on a gorgeous mezzanine, a giftwrap desk, and
a branch of B. Dalton Books right on the premises.

Clothing is a special attraction at A & S, as evi-
denced by its teens, juniors, young men, and careerists
divisions, all spaciously arranged with the idea that you
need not crowd the shopper to get them to buy something.
See chapter 13, "Womenswear."

W.C. ART & DRAFTING SUPPLY CO.
375 Jay Street
Downtown Brooklyn, take "A/C/F" to Jay Street,
Borough Hall
718/855-8078
American Express, MC, Visa, checks
Closed Sunday

You can buy all the supplies you need at W.C. if
you're a graphic designer—and even a few crucial things
if you just write in a notebook. Like many of the stores in
the neighborhood, W.C. will be moving in 1991 to the
Metro-tech complex being built for all the downtown
Brooklyn mainstays. For now, W.C. has been moved to a
smaller space so, unfortunately, much of their stock isn't
here. But still, you will find all the basic supplies, such as
markers, pens, paper goods, a wide selection of portfolios
and envelopes, commercial stationery, Letraset press-let-
ters, and specialty items for illustrators and designers. All
of this is priced slightly above wholesale.

Drafting tables, cabinets, tables and chairs, desk
lamps, and other fine furniture, all at very good prices,
can be purchased in a little-known showroom housed in a
nearby ancient firehouse (located at 365 Jay Street). That
small showroom has remained a big secret since W.C.
moved out of its first store; you would do well to be one
of the few to take advantage of its low prices.

GEM PAWNBROKERS
378 Schermerhorn Street
Downtown Brooklyn, take "2/3/4/5/D/Q" to
Atlantic Avenue
718/596-LOAN
American Express, MC, Visa
Closed Sunday

Unlike Manhattan's lowly pawn shops, Brooklyn's Gem hosts affordable secondhand jewelry, typewriters, T.V. sets (ancient black-and-whites are in at the Gem), musical instruments, and all sorts of assorted household goods in decent condition.

The guys who work at Gem are eager to help. Ask them about their selection and don't be surprised if they move from behind the counter to show you, by playing the baby cello, saxophone, guitar, harmonicas, or drums. Based on the demonstration I got, I have a hunch they're all musicians.

STANDARD EQUIPMENT
3175 Fulton Street
Downtown Brooklyn, take "A/C/G" to
Hoyt-Schermerhorn Streets
718/235-4440
No credit cards
Closed Sunday

Standard has a catalogue filled with new, used, surplus, and reconditioned office furniture. Prices are up to 60 percent off retail and they are happy to talk about their product line on the phone. (Most phone-sales companies won't talk to you unless you have an exact model number and make.) This firm makes all kinds of industrial-quality chairs, stools, shelving, bins, filing cabinets, desks, and other industrial supplies. Most things are best suited to large businesses or home workshops. But they tell me you can take one of their rather dingy-looking metal cabinets, add a dab of spray paint, and have a beautiful, modern accessory for your home.

This place is not for you if you think shopping means walking into a store and being greeted by, "May I help you?" They are not used to walk-in customers and aren't particularly solicitous. But at least ask for a catalogue; you never know when you might want to turn one of Standard's polyethylene "barrels" into a cheap, and noiseless, trash can.

UTRECHT MANUFACTURING COMPANY
33 35th Street
Downtown Brooklyn, take "A/C/F" to Jay Street,
Borough Hall
718/768-2525
MC, Visa, checks
Closed Saturday and Sunday

Utrecht has been selling supplies to professional artists, sculptors, and printers since 1949. The company manufactures and distributes the best-priced oil and acrylic paints available, and the store has all the other necessary equipment, including canvas, stretchers, frames, pads, paper, brushes, tools, books, easels, tables, pigments, palettes, solvents, and even more. Utrecht's several lines are in stock, as are Pentel, Niji, and others. The catalogue is huge, and they offer discounts of 5–30 percent on already low prices when you buy in quantity.

STEREO/VIDEO WAREHOUSE
2377 Flatbush Avenue
Flatbush, Brooklyn, take "4/5" to Flatbush Avenue
718/253-8804
American Express, MC, Visa
Closed Sunday

Although I rarely suggest shopping in chain stores,

here I make an exception: The Stereo Warehouse store on Flatbush Avenue—unlike the one on Manhattan's West 57th Street and those in upstate New York, in New Jersey, and on Long Island—is a spectacular place to buy stereo equipment. It makes good sense to go to a place that handles everything, and here you'll fine BIC, Dual, Teac, Bose, Onkyo, Technics, Aiwa, Akai, Shure, Marantz, Pioneer, Kenwood, Sony, Harman Kardon, Sansui, TDK, and Yamaha all under the same roof.

Because Stereo Warehouse is not beholden to any particular brand, they aren't pushing you toward one or another. I find this low-pressure environment a great place to browse for equipment. They sell everything under the sun, including a fine line of unusual turntables. Since they are displaying so much stock, the sales clerks are unusually willing to make deals.

You need makes and model numbers of many different pieces of equipment before you can actually decide on something. So you might as well go to a place that has everything on hand. (The Manhattan store is well stocked, too, but the prices are a little higher.) See chapter 20, "Home Appliances."

SID'S HARDWARE
345 Jay Street
Downtown Brooklyn, take "A/C/F" to Jay Street,
Borough Hall
718/875-2259
American Express, MC, Visa, checks

A thirteen thousand square-feet environment is a nice place to wander into when you need hardware supplies. The fifty-seven-year-old Sid's, run by a guy named Hymie, is the one place everyone in the downtown area goes for their home improvement needs. Say you want a do-it-yourself wall or fireplace. Sit down with Hymie or one of the guys and work out the entire process—he'll cut it and have it shipped to you pronto. The prices are more than reasonable. Hymie says it's because "We know our competition only too well: we do our pricing depending on how much items are being sold for elsewhere."

Products include bolts, nails, screws by the point, electrical equipment, hand and power tools, janitorial supplies, paint, lumber, plywood, molding, paneling, wallpaper, cabinets, shutters, everything. They offer free delivery if you buy in quantity. Hymie calls it "the home of a million items." Others may boast the same, but if you can't find it here, really do ask for it. Most likely, if it's hardware, its stored away somewhere.

Sid's is moving to nearby Metro-tech Center in 1991, as are most of the shops around here, where they will have a brand-new store for the first time in 60 years.

E.B.A. WHOLESALERS
2361 Nostrand Avenue
Flatbush, Brooklyn, take "2/5" to Flatbush Avenue
718/252-3400
MC, Visa

Sold at discount prices that beat all others in Manhattan and Brooklyn, the T.V.s, refrigerators, microwaves, and washer-dryers are in good company at E.B.A. There are 3000 square feet filled with major brands, and a no-nonsense attitude about discounts. They will, says the manager, sell anything to you at less than what you'll find it for elsewhere—just quote a price if you know the model number.

E.B.A. is not Crazy Eddie: E.B.A. will never steer you to a more expensive make that you don't need. The staff is extremely knowledgeable about their products, which makes this a perfect place to go just to browse. See chapter 20, "Home Appliances."

MARIE'S CERAMIC WORLD
1818 Flatbush Avenue
Flatbush, Brooklyn, take "2/5" to Flatbush Avenue
718/951-8421
Closed Friday, Sunday, and Monday

This is an unusual way to get ceramic vases, figurines, pitchers, small animal pieces, and just about anything that would come in a clay mold. At Marie's you do half the work. Spend a few dollars on the clay molds—she buys each piece individually—plus a few dollars on the paint, and then a few dollars more for the paint brush. After that, you work with Marie in a free class on finishing that priceless item. You do everything except the firing—Marie does that after you leave. Then you come back a few days later and—presto!—your work is done. "You make your mess here," says Marie. Fine, because you pay about half the price that you would at a boutique.

BARCLAY SCHOOL SUPPLIES
166 Livingston Street
Downtown Brooklyn, take "2/3/4/5" to Borough Hall
718/875-2424
American Express, MC, Visa, checks
Closed Sunday

Billed as a "toy store," this educational supply company houses hundreds of discounted educational supplies that you can purchase at a fraction of what they cost in the catalogue. Although Barclay has offices throughout much of this building, go to the third-floor showroom and see flash cards, posters, duplicating books, manipulative skill-enhancers, easels, bulletin boards, chalkboard erasers, study materials such as computer software, and as a spokeswoman put it, "anything for the child or person who wants to learn—but no guns or war games." They also carry office supplies at major discounts—anything your firm might need, with convenient financing negotiable.

At last look, Barclay, which is nearly 40 years old, had branched out to offer a wide range of comparably priced furniture in a special office furnishings division, including desks and a full line of cabinets. Barclay is a one-stop place for the educator and very much worth the while of anyone who works at a desk.

BINKIN'S BOOK STORE
54 Willoughby Street
Downtown Brooklyn, take "A/C/F" to Jay Street,
Borough Hall
718/855-7813
No credit cards
Closed Sunday

Here's where readers get their just deserts in Brooklyn: Binkin's is the oldest bookstore in the borough, and you can find numerous titles, paperback and leather-bound: rare editions, books on New York City, black history, art, novels, and mysteries. The only thing is, all selections are dated. Upstairs is a collection of rare books. They sell all paperbacks at half the suggested price. For charm, there's a garden in the back with some 50 feet to sit and spend a few minutes with a book before you buy it.

AVERY BOOK STORE
308 Livingston Street
Downtown Brooklyn, take "A/C/G" to Hoyt,
Schermerhorn Streets
718/858-3606
American Express
Closed Sunday

Avery features used books and magazines and boasts

an extraordinary selection of Modern Library editions, travel, Brooklyn and Long Island history, and feminist books. Their prices are not as low as Binkin's, but their selection is no doubt unique. It's the kind of shop that can always surprise the finicky reader.

CHAPTER 10

Upstate World

WOODBURY COMMON

I have to give the decade-old Woodbury Common an A-plus for setting and shopping grounds. Located right off the New York State Thruway, you'll see it just off exit 16 at the junction of Routes 87 and 17. Don't miss this place if you are a serious shopper.

Many people swear by their monthly or biannual treks to Woodbury because of the footwear, men's and women's wear, housewares, and accessory shops. The large factory warehouses make shopping terrific fun. You can find everything here in a matter of hours.

This and the Flemington Liberty Village (See chapter 6, "New Jersey") are built by the same parent company, but this is the cleaner and more old-fashioned of the two. Nestled in the foothills of the gorgeous Catskill Mountains, it's a beautiful sight year round. Customers come back in part because, unlike other planned communities, the pastel-colored buildings that zigzag the street make the place feel like a small town! Be sure you go on a weekday, because weekends are treacherous—more people than on a giveaway day at Shea.

Van Heusen Factory Store sells first quality, in-fashion merchandise for men and women at 25 to 60 percent off suggested retail prices. **Alice's Wonderland** offers children's knickknacks for but a few pennies, and you can even find teddy bears for $2! The **Corning Factory Store** (see below for Corning, New York) has big savings on Corning, Pyrex, Corelle, and Visions replacement parts and discount product overstocks.

Hamilton Watch Factory offers the best deals on grandfather clocks and Swatches. (Note their exchange policy whereby you can trade in old watches for cash.) **Socks Plus** is the cheapest I've seen for nightshirts, crew, knit, and runaround socks, and particularly "executive footwear" at $3–$4. Knee-highs are sold in mix-and-match, too. **Royal House** has discount sterling silver jewelry, Benrus watches, sunglasses, souvenirs, T-shirts, and a wide assortment of gift cards. **Bass Shoe** has a 25 percent savings on Weejuns, Sunjuns, and other sandals. **Carter's Childrenswear** sells nationally known children's clothing featuring the Carter's label, including layette, infants, toddlers, and boy's and girl's sizes 4–14. **Athletic Outlet** has a savings of up to 60 percent on sneakers and active apparel for men, women, and kids. **Jindo Furs** is at this writing the world's largest manufacturer of furs and leathers. They also have a full line of coats and accessories, and a host of men's items. (See chapter 11, "Outerwear.") **Royal Doulton** stocks fine English dinnerware and giftware at great savings. The **Harvé Benard** shop has a wide selection of women's and men's designer apparel and accessories at dramatic savings.

Other great bargains can be found at **Rosenbaum Jewelry**, with a wide assortment of diamond brooches; a large shop called **Eklektic Designer Dreams** for misses' clothing; an **Anne Klein** with a limited but stylish selection of petites; and a full-time open stock sale at **Liz Claiborne**. In the Claiborne outlet, there is a placard that wisely suggests you "look for last year's models here and shop your favorite department store for the newest Claiborne fashions."

You'll find the following unusual events going on in and around Woodbury: A food court comprising over 8 eateries, such as a tiny, friendly, Italian cafeteria-restaurant, a croissanterie, and of course **McDonald's**. (The whole court is a very uncomplicated place to eat.) The **Gourmet Basket** is a hybrid of stores: chocolates, soup mixes, toppings, natural extracts, blue corn popcorn and other unusual snacks, and lingonberries, just for starters. The **New York Farm** market sells tulips, daffodils, hyacinths, azaleas, and mums. They hold a biannual flower festival that is fun to gaze at, and they sell terrific spring produce from March through June in addition to year-round homemade pies, fresh bread, cheese, maple syrup, and scrumptious varieties of honey.

The luxurious **Dansk Factory Warehouse** is filled with oddities unexpected at a factory outlet, such as hurricane lamps, candlesticks, Kobenstyle stoveware with teak handles, and a great assortment of oven-fired clay espresso cups. Many people are also surprised by the overfilled **American Tourister** showroom (one of the largest of its kind in the country) with values that might put people in shock: quality luggage sold as sets and pieces, starting at $39.99—suggested retail price $100. The business case selection features the French West Indies brand.

I mention the **Manhattan Factory Store** last because it is something really unusual. This place has up to 60 percent specials on men's and women's fashions—with hourly closeouts on certain racks. While Manhattan Factory Store has outlets all over the country, most of its branches sell a *particular* line of clothing. This one sells everything they can get hold of: Perry Ellis American, Manhattan Shirt, Big & Tall Shirts, Peters/Ashley, Henry Grethel, Vera for women, Lady Manhattan, and Lucinda Rhodes. It's quite a shopping trip, even for the seasoned (or jaded) shopper.

For more information on Woodbury, call the customer service bureau controlling the goings-on in Central Valley at 914/928-6840. American Express, MC, and Visa are accepted in all stores. During the months of May through December, expect all of Woodbury Common's stores to be open until 9 p.m. on Thursday and Friday evenings.

LATHAM OUTLET VILLAGE

Located in Latham on the corners of Routes 9 and 9R, the actual address is 400 Old Loudon Road. You can see it from the highway that leads you to it: Take Route 87 to exit 7 and it's right there.

There are bus tours to this beautiful village in the mountains. You can take a bus here from the Port Authority (212/564-8484) and even make your way around the village via small van.

What's here? **Van Heusen Factory Store** has first quality fashion apparel for men and women at 25–60 percent off. This place is operated by the Phillips Van Heusen Corp., which means you're getting new, fine-quality manufactured goods. **Aileen Factory Outlet** has savings of up to 70 percent on women's separates, coordinates, and sportswear. **Liza's Plus Fashions** advertises truly "value, variety, and versatility" in dressing full-figured women. The **Lenox Factory Shop** has up to 60 percent on seconds of Lenox china, stemware, and other gift products. **Harvé**

Benard is another fine collection of the famed designer's products, this time with a 40 percent markdown on dresses, coats, accessories, and beautiful sportswear suits for women (and jackets for men).

In addition, find **Oneida Factory Store's** savings on stainless and silverplated flatware, and baby gift items; the **Colonial Sportshoe Center** athletic apparel and shoes at outlet prices; and **The Statuary's** wall art by Austin, with ceramics, lathe art, pedestals, and cast paper, at 20 percent off regular prices.

The number for further information is 518/785-8200. All stores are open seven days and accept American Express, MC, and Visa. Ask them to send you a kit that details both present and planned stores.

ROCHESTER

I was so impressed with the amount of merchandise you could find in this small city, I took two trips to Rochester. From glassware and china to clothing and art, this is one town every adamant shopper should visit at least once.

Unlike Woodbury and Latham, stores here are not in one central location. On West Henrietta Road in the middle of Rochester find **Clothes Works** (3333 West Henrietta Road, 716/424-7222, American Express, Visa) selling famous women's designers at 20 percent off. As this book went to press, this block had other small shops coming onto the scene.

The famous **Glass Factory Outlet** (Ridge Road, 716/225-4763, American Express, MC, Visa, closed some Sundays) sells a whole assortment of glass pieces and knicknacks, and is a glass lover's delight. They call it, "The Glass Gift Place": you can't go wrong if gifts are your thing. (Glass aficionados should see "Corning," below.)

To get to Rochester, take I-90 to Exit 46, "Route 15 and Route 390." Take 390 to Exit 14. The Henrietta Plaza is close by. Also, Route 390 holds many factory stores.

CORNING

If you're a glass person, or simply interested in a good price on practical home accessories, you should take a one or two-day trip to picturesque Corning, New York, where everything for the shopper is within a few blocks' walking distance. The **Corning Glass Works Factory** (Route 17, 607/874-8271, MC and Visa) has a museum with unusual exhibits pertaining to the making of glass objects. And find substantial savings on Visions, Corning Ware, Corelle, Pyrex, Revere, microwave cookware, and kitchen accessories at the factory store next door. Discontinued patterns and products are featured every day. This store ships nationwide, so you can stock up here.

Get to Corning by taking Route 17 to Corning Glass Works on Center Way—signs are everywhere you look. Also, take a tour of the **Steuben Glass Factory** on Center Way; for $4 you get an hour-long demonstration of the manufacture of fine Steuben Glass. A large **Corning Factory Store** (114 Pine Street, 607/974-4343, American Express, MC, Visa) is also nearby.

At last look, Corning had become quite a factory outlet center, with kids' clothing stores, shirt outlets by **Van Heusen**, the **Manhattan Factory Outlet** (see above), and the kitchen accessory outlet **Fieldcrest Cannon Factory Outlet** (21 West Market Street, 607/936-6371, American Express, MC, Visa). All of these are on East and West Market Streets, right by Center Way.

Call Corning's public information representatives at 607/974-8271.

CHAPTER 11

Outerwear

JINDO FURS
41 West 57th Street, 754-1177; Closed Sunday in spring and summer
1010 Third Avenue, 754-1166; Closed Sunday
575 Fifth Avenue, 3rd Level Atrium, 867-0710; Closed Sunday
American Express, MC, Visa

Jindo is a Korean-based furrier with stores in most major cities. Expect to find a general 20 to 50 percent off regular prices of coats that include mink with fox trim, natural and dyed furs, and minks for every season. They have good leather selection, too, but the prices are better at leather shops.

One interesting thing about these warehouses is that they do not appear to be discount houses—they display the higher priced items as you enter—but as you wander into the back you will notice racks of bargain items to make all fur shoppers' days.

Jindo has inexpensive storage capabilities, too, and at the end of the winter season their storage prices have come down as low as $19.95. They offer a Club Plan for $97.50, an "annual fur package" for fur lovers. Jindo is also located at **Woodbury Common** in Central Valley, 914/928-9953, and the **Designer Outlet Center** in Secaucus, New Jersey, 201/330-9777.

A & M FURS
129 West 30th Street
279-2117
American Express
Closed Saturday and Sunday

A & M has one of the most extraordinary collections of racoon jackets, coats, and strollers in regular and petite sizes. Styles include unique silhouettes with workmanship prized by their customers. They also stock a fine selection of men's furs, and hold great seasonal sample sales.

FIN FUR
214 West 29th Street
465-0767
No credit cards
Closed Saturday and Sunday

You should make an appointment before coming into Fin. This is a manufacturer of fine leather and fur garments—jackets, coats, and full-length furs. You can get any size, and bargain with them for a fair price (do some shopping beforehand).

HARRY KIRSCHNER AND SONS
307 Seventh Avenue, 4th Floor
243-4847
American Express, MC, Visa
Closed Sunday

If you love coats, then get yours here. You can find sales before the season begins (see Introduction for more on seasons) and in the summer months they will actually sell some at cost. The designers include Lanvin, Dior, Carole Little, Valentino, and Nina Ricci. I especially like their throw pillows made of fine fur, and the fact that even though everyone's so busy here, they will take time to give you a tour of the factory if you ask. See chapter 23, "Those Answered Questions."

GOLDIN FELDMAN FURS
345 Seventh Avenue, 12th Floor
594-4415
American Express, MC, Visa
Closed Saturday and Sunday

Find top designers' furs at wholesale prices. See chapter 3, "Sample Sales."

P. MILLER AND SON
307 Seventh Avenue, Room 602
242-8688
Checks accepted
Closed Sunday

The Millers manufacture fine furs and have special sales year round. You can get mink, fox, unplucked beaver, coyote, swakara, and other luxurious furs. They have special assorted jackets off the rack—often with extra-special prices on one-shots—from many distributors that they work with. An accessory division is here too, offering hats, scarves, headbands, and fur earmuffs. All sizes are available.

RONLEE
32 West 36th Street, 4th Floor
695-3481
American Express, MC, Visa
Closed Sunday

This fur manufacturer claims to sell furs at a smidgen above cost: full-lengths of mink, beaver, raccoon, fox, and coyote at low, low prices. They have children's selections and raincoats, both starting at $75. You can buy a new, fine fur for just $750 here. They also have a Secaucus outlet (124 Enterprise Avenue South, 342-1200, extension 424) where they sell leather coats at 20 percent above cost. See chapter 6, "New Jersey."

LORD & TAYLOR CLEARANCE CENTER
839-16 New York Avenue, Huntington, Long Island
516/673-0009
Lord & Taylor Charge

Here's where Lord & Taylor unloads everything the managers in individual stores can't find the room for. See this as a golden opportunity: everything in outerwear is at the closeout center. Since it's open seven days you can even make a weekend outing of it. The selections include raincoats, good leather jackets starting at $50, some furs that you can use on not-so-special occasions, and especially children's coats in sizes preadolescent to teen. On a recent journey, I found that you can get anything here at about 50 percent off retail stores' prices. For anyone who's ever shopped at a Lord & Taylor, that's something to be seen.

I, MICHAEL
1041 Madison Avenue, 2nd Floor
737-7273
MC, Visa
Closed Sunday

Though a place that specializes in resale gowns, you can also find a great selection of off-price jackets for women. See chapter 13, "Womenswear."

THE LIGHTHOUSE FOR THE BLIND
11 East 59th Street
355-2200
American Express, checks

This worthy association throws a party twice a year called the PoshSale that is an inexpensive way to buy women's leather, furs, and rain gear. You can come for a whole week during October or April, and feast on a wide selection of fine goods, donated by women from all over the country. Proceeds benefit the Lighthouse.

CENTURY 21 DEPARTMENT STORES
12 Cortlandt Street off Broadway by
World Trade Center
227-9092
American Express, MC, Visa, checks
Closed Sunday (Saturday in July and August)

Don't miss out on the merchandise at Century 21, which is an amazing store for womenswear and menswear. (For the entire scoop on Century 21, see chapter 8, "Brooklyn the Eclectic.")

An inordinately large section of the store is filled with overcoats; it specializes in women's designer coats and men's sports jackets. The savings on rain gear and outerwear are phenomenal. It's even better than men's discounters **Sym's** (nearby location is 45 Park Place, 791-1199), who advertise that "An educated consumer is our best customer" and confuse people with their pricing strategy. (See chapter 12, "Menswear.") Sym's markup is higher than Century 21's by 20 to 40 percent.

ABE GELLER
141 West 36th Street, 9th Floor
736-8077
No credit cards; checks and money orders accepted
Closed Sunday

Having moved to a larger showroom, Mr. Geller's has some of the best upscale coats and raincoats in town. Although much of what they sell is expensive, they do discount an item 30 to 40 percent after it has been sitting for a few months. Abe's is closed most of July.

GENE LONDON PRODUCTIONS
897 Broadway
533-4105
Closed Saturday and Sunday

You must make an appointment to come to London's, the boutique that helps outfit major and independent motion pictures. However, inquire about their special sales open to the general public; there you can get "old glamour," as they say, from ancient films, and a few from recent days, too. The best is their selection of coats made as period pieces for Garbo, Crawford, and other movie queens.

There are some 3,000 garments, and some of them will only cost you $100. It's best to go here when you have a lot of time on your hands. You never know what you'll find if you browse long enough. Call them up about special floor model sales.

BOGIE'S ANTIQUE FURS AND CLOTHING
201 East 10th Street
260-1199
No credit cards
Closed Sunday, and Saturday in summer

This small store caters to people who want old furs and old dresses, and leather coats in small sizes. Also, take yours here if you need immediate repairs (they do it on the premises). This store is an amazing "trash shop"; that is, clothes are piled everywhere, in spite of the work they put into it to keep the merchandise moving. And to keep things moving they keep the prices low. It's hard to say what will be here at any given time, but in six visits over the last year I found leather jackets hanging at Bogie's for as little as $75. And as leather shops disappear as fast as I can find them, it's important to note that Bogie's is still around. When last I called them, they told me, "We're still here, but all our clothes are getting older!"

PIERRE FURS
224 West 30th Street
244-3790
American Express, MC, Visa

While many furs need repair, fixing them can often be very expensive. Here's a place that has a strict pricing policy—*cheap!* If you bring in an old coat, their designers will repair it with "new style and fit." They claim to buy and sell remodeled furs, although I've never seen an old one for sale. (Buying remodels can save you hundreds of dollars, but only do it if you're looking for a coat to get you through a single season.) See coupon in back for $20 off your personal remodels.

For more on leather fashions, see chapter 7, "Best of Orchard Street."

CHAPTER 12

Menswear

This is the chapter men should study, particularly those who want to dress better. And "better," in this case, does not mean "more expensively." It means finding stores that do not overcharge for fine and casual clothing.

Note that the two most popular stores for suits (Sym's and N.B.O.) are not featured in this chapter. Both marts are examples of chain stores that advertise a far better quality than what they possess, and both use an antiquated markdown strategy—the older an item gets, the cheaper. I prefer to depend on low prices that are *stable*. Information is provided here, however, because the stores do have low-priced merchandise: **Sym's** ("An Educated Consumer Is Our Best Customer"), 45 Park Place, 792-1199; American Express, MC, Visa; closed Saturday. **N.B.O.** is National Brands Outlet ("Life Is Hard, N.B.O. Is Easy"), 1965 Broadway, 595-1550; American Express, MC, Visa).

If you are a man's size 28–30, be sure to check out the young men's sections at large department stores, for they offer discounts for late teens and young adults that you can fit into. If you have misgivings about doing this, just remember, you're always a kid inside.

WEISS AND MAHONEY
142 Fifth Avenue
American Express, MC, Visa
Closed Sunday

The owners call this "the peaceful little Army and Navy store" and sell a wide array of inexpensive jeans, military clothing, and uniforms. You can find field jackets, leather bomber jackets, and even a $70 pea coat. I was amazed with the many different pieces made from denim: a hat, a shirt, a cap, even dress pants! The prices for these range from $10–$30. Levi's, Lee, Dee Cee, and the no-name brands sit together in the form of straight and baggy jeans, painter pants, and fatigue outfits. (For more, see chapter 1, "Shoes!")

Recommended army-navy stores include **New York Army-Navy** (328 Bleecker Street, 242-6665; 221 East 59th Street, 755-1855; 118 Eighth Avenue, 645-7420; and 1598 Second Avenue, 737-4661). Another is **Dave's Army & Navy Store** (779 Sixth Avenue, 989-6444). Lastly, if you're in the area, try **Soho Surplus** (594 Broadway, 334-9771) and **Hudson's** (97 Third Avenue, 463-0981). All the above stores accept American Express, MC, and Visa.

L.B.C. CLOTHING
337 Grand Street
226-1620
American Express, MC, Visa
Closed Sunday

One of the Lower East Side's greatest finds for men's

clothing is little-known L.B.C. Unlike other stores where you have to wait for a special sale, the savings on suits and sports clothing here are a constant: This is a warehouse outlet, meaning their stockrooms are overflowing with merchandise and they have to make space available by lowering prices.

Walk into the shop and you'll be surprised, because it doesn't seem a likely place to find a large stock at great discounts. But within the modest interior is a great selection of suits, raincoats, slacks, and coats. L.B.C. features the same fine quality merchandise that the next three places I mention sell at top prices. Here, however, the prices are slashed by between 40 and 60 percent. Often the discounts are higher on irregular pieces.

THREE PLACES TO SEE SUITS

- ◆ **Rothman's** (200 Park Avenue South, 777-7400; American Express, MC, Visa) is a newfangled warehouse store in the refurbished center of Union Square. It's run by the grandnephew of famous entrepreneur Harry Rothman, who once employed finicky tailors in a huge warehouse on Fifth Avenue who helped you choose bargain-basement clothing. (If you want that Old World style, try **Lesh Clothing Company**, 115 Fifth Avenue, 6th floor, 255-6893; American Express, MC; closed Saturday).

  Times have changed, and new owner Kenny still has 30–70 percent savings on suits, shirts, ties, and accessories, though the atmosphere is much calmer. Constant sales bring imported suits down to a notch above wholesale.

- ◆ **A. Rubinstein & Sons** (63 East Broadway, 226-9696; American Express, MC, Visa; closed Saturday). About ninety years ago, this man's store stood in the middle of a Jewish mecca. Today it's in Chinatown—

)instein's former clothing junk shop now sells
ts, formal wear, topcoats, and coats with de-
e linings. He and his sons have stock that is
pricey, but it's constantly being closed out at
∠∪ ₋ercent off their prices. Don't expect to be a
cheapskate, though. Classy shirts start at $40–$50,
decent jackets at around $100.

◆ **Merns Mart,** formerly Merns (2 West 46th Street; 1
Vesey Street; 227-5471; American Express, MC,
Visa) was, at press time, holding a long-running
"going out of business" sale that looked to outlast
"A Chorus Line." Pay no mind, though, because
dress shirts, casual slacks, dress slacks, tuxedo parts,
poplins, and sportcoats are still being priced well below normal retail. Brands featured are Polo, Chaps,
Marzott, Adolfo, Birtolini, Givenchy, Cassini, Dela-
cort, and Bugle Boy Men's. The Young Men's department beats almost all others.

CANAL JEAN'S
504 Broadway
226-1140
American Express, MC, Visa

If you like punk, antique, or just good old-fashioned
American clothing, Canal's the place to wander through.
Clerks walk around chewing gum and showing off their
odd hats; and they will also help you find clothing. There
are T-shirts, carpenter pants, safety jeans, belts, jackets in
all makes and styles, and even a special overcoat section
with prices that start at $15! Try a tie on, or just look at
yourself in a pair of overalls! They sell M-65s and other
army wear right by the bins overflowing with painters'
clothing (very fashionable indeed). Cotton turtlenecks are
$4–$15 and, yes, Canal Jeans start at $10. Find designer
jeans way in the back—as if they were being disavowed.

They once had the main Canal Jeans outlet on Canal Street, but they have consolidated all their wares—including jewelry, fashion pins, and a host of baseball and other hats—in one trilevel store. The savings are especially good for men; the bins outside the store are stocked with fun throwaway clothing (you have to look closely to find your size and color), and their new second floor is devoted to men's fashions. Prices at Canal are so low you will think you've returned to yesterday. Yet the clothing styles are pure '90s.

FOWAD
2554 Broadway
222-6000
American Express, MC, Visa

At Fowad, you will be overwhelmed by the amount of merchandise. And you will be underwhelmed by the determinedly unfriendly service! But their self-described "clothing market" has good savings on casual clothing. (It's actually an upscale version of the **Gap;** see chapter 14, "Children's Wear.") They have a decent dress shirt selection including specially tagged "imported fitted shirts" at $19.99. Also find socks, bathing suits, a rack of closeout suits, sports jackets, unusual leather belts, and rack upon rack of designer silk ties. Names include Dior, Ellis, Cardin, and obscure Italian designers like Nervurina, Riccardo, and Giovanni.

A $45 Pierre Cardin sports jacket was spotted there recently, as were several $9.99 Armani ties and a tie-dyed bathing suit in 14 colors for $11.99. Fowad is certainly worth a stop by, even if Broadway has, in the '90s, become the neighborhood to shop. New stores are opening up every month.

As I walked out of the store on an early spring day, I noticed the owners setting up bins outside, à la Canal Jeans. Inside those compartments they were placing quality white and new-design T-shirts for $11.99. If that sounds like a lot for a simple "T," keep in mind that the poorly constructed ones fall apart with a few washings. Sturdy, all-cotton shirts are worth a few bucks more. And while we're on the subject, if you seek tank tops or simple white shirts, go to **Eisner Brothers** (76 Orchard Street, 475-6868; American Express, MC, Visa; closed Saturday), where you can find a rainbow of "T" colors and many novelty shirts. (They'll expedite mail orders, too.)

LEWIS & CLARK/EXPLORER'S COMPANY
228 Seventh Avenue; 751 Broadway; 27 Seventh Avenue; 115 West Broadway
255-4686 (254-6534 for 751 Broadway)

One of my favorite places to shop, their slogan, "A store for men to explore," tells it all. These boutiques must hire managers wth short attention spans, because whenever a rack of men's casual clothing (ties, jeans, shirts, corduroys, linen and denim jackets, and more) has been standing around for a few days, the prices drop by around 30 percent. And the manager moves the rack closer to the entrance!

Unlike department stores that hide their best bargains in the back, Lewis & Clark/Explorer's Company wants you to get right away how great their prices are. So the tags keep sliding down on slacks, rugby shirts, dress shirts, sweaters, cardigan shirts, and socks. Here is a place where a man can shop successfully, even if he is—gasp!— an uneducated consumer.

Another decent example of this pricing methodology is **Dollar Bill's** (99 East 42nd Street, 867-0212; American Express, MC, Visa), a department store with good men's clothing at low prices. Unlike Lewis/Explorer's, which needs to move goods quickly in order to restock the shelves, Bill's buys clothing in bulk and passes these "bulk

discounts" on to customers in a wide variety of sportjackets, slacks, shirts, and ties. Find several racks of non-designer jeans all priced under $25.

ALICE UNDERGROUND
Best store: 481 Broadway, 431-9067
Branch: 380 Columbus Avenue, 724-6682
Checks accepted with proper I.D.

I must recommend Alice as the lady to see if you are
in the market for a second-hand shirt in good condition
by Christian Dior, Ralph Lauren, Brooks Brothers, Perry
Ellis, or Calvin Klein (off-color varieties such as baby blue
or pink). Shirts cost between $8 and $15 and bow ties in
a myriad of pastels and darks are only $3. Recently, I saw
Auzi trousers and extra-small army shirts for $10, and a
so-called "hippie shirt" for $15.

Two maitre d's I know buy silk jackets for $12; their
After Six dinner jackets for $15; and all their white shirts
for about $10. The old clothes are in impeccable shape
here, unlike other places that advertise "resale" and really
sell junk.

In the neighborhood: **Mano a Mano** (580 Broadway,
219-9602; American Express, MC, Visa) sells you "indi-
vidualistic sportswear" at good prices—socks, ties, belts,
slacks, and summer and winter suits. Most of the merchandise is imported from Italy, though a great deal of
their summer wear is merely shoddily manufactured.
There are $100 silk suits, and many of their pants are
sold at prices remarkably labeled, "$24 each, two for
$39." Conclusion: Fine Prago tweed blazers are a steal at
"$29 each, two for $48," but don't bother with the flimsy
shirts by Savile Row ($15). You can have fun in the sun
with $20 sunglasses, and they usually sell Multo Uomo
sporty trousers for $39–$49. Plus, watch music videos
while you shop.

See **Cheap Jack's** (845 Broadway, 777-9564; American Express, MC, Visa) for "vintage clothing" and inexpensive, fun tuxedo parts that are in excellent shape. Buying tuxedos one piece at a time—tie, cumberbund, shirt, pants—saves money. They also have "funky shirts," slacks, and bow ties that are priceless and priced low, along with nice, helpful people who talk to you about the newest fads, listen to '60s music, and decorate their store as if it were in a time warp. Automatic discounts are given with an in-store coupon found at the front counter.

THRIFT SHOPS

Most thrift places and clothing bazaars sell womenswear. But in these places men can do quite well:

♦ **Exchange Unlimited** (563 Second Avenue, 889-3229; checks accepted with proper I.D.; closed Sunday) is a resale shop for "very special things," and while resale is known as a womenswear term meaning "secondhand," Exchange comes through for men, too. Expect to run into new-looking outfits such as Perry Ellis jackets, pants, and sweaters. After thirty days, they reduce the already low prices an additional 30 percent; then 50 percent after sixty days; and 75 percent after a season (ninety days).

♦ **Everybody's Thrift Shop** (261 Park Avenue South, 355-9263; closed Sunday) has an incredible array of men's overcoats and eclectic, unstained, ready-to-wear jackets. I was told that clothing is not the norm here—that small furniture and other knickknacks are. I don't buy it. Instead I bought one tweed sportjacket, a double-breasted Irish suitcoat, and an oversized raincoat in blue!

MOE GINSBURG
162 Fifth Avenue
242-3482
American Express, MC, Visa

"The name in New York for better clothing" is the slogan at Moe's. This outlet on Fifth stands in the middle of a series of buildings where you can shop for men's suits all day. (For the story on lower Fifth Avenue, see chapter 25, "Unnoticed Areas.") But why bother scavenging around when you can come to four floors of Moe Ginsburg and find name-brand classic designer suits and all the necessary accessories. The American suits start at just over $100, (third floor) and the Europeans, racks and racks of them, begin at just $200 (fifth floor). Also find socks, silk ties, underwear, belts, and suspenders (accessories, second floor); a huge selection of slacks, sportscoats, rainwear and complete tuxedos (extras, fourth floor), and all of this at impressive savings. Moe Ginsburg certifies as a one-stop place for men.

You can rely on the sales clerks, who don't work on commission and therefore aren't pushy. A recent sale exemplifies their bargains: Thousands of Italian suits on the fifth floor were reduced from over $600 to $290 each; and suits on the third floor made of wools, midweights and tropicals, in athletic fit, were slashed dramatically to $160–$260.

GILCREST-TOWNSMAN CLOTHES CO.
900 Broadway, 3rd Floor
254-8933
American Express, MC, Visa

Here's a place to shop if you hate to shop: one floor only, with racks of good suits, all priced between $319 and $339 for the imported variety (Ellis, Lanvin, Adolfo, Julian), and $239 and $279 for domestic brands specially woven for the Gilcrest label. It's a simple process with no pricetags and no fast-talking. The salespeople at Gilcrest want to please you, so they would never push you to buy a suit, but unlike at Moe Ginsburg, they do work on commission. First thing they'll tell you—all alterations are free.

You will also find a fine selection of raincoats for $399 (Dupont manufactured, Gilcrest tag), and a very appealing tie rack with imported silks for $25 and a collection crafted for Gilcrest for $20.

The dress shirt collection is mostly manufactured by Damon and not terribly interesting. For those, high-tail it to Moe's. They also have in their stock a large number of overpriced tuxedos. Again, buy your tuxedos in pieces. (See **Cheap Jack's**, above.)

Still, if shopping is not your favorite hobby, come to Gilcrest, where you could spend an afternoon talking suits with a clerk. One recently suggested that, "Anyone who comes here once, comes back for life." At press time they were adding 25 percent more space to this already well-stocked showroom.

In the same neighborhood, try **Fenwick Clothes** (22 West 19th Street, 243-1100; American Express, MC, Visa; closed Saturday). This factory showroom offers 40 percent discounts on suits and sportjackets. See coupon in the back.

L.S. CLOTHING
19 West 44th Street, Room 403
575-0933
Closed Saturday (open Sunday by appointment)

"The first name in traditional menswear" is what this conservative store calls itself. It's not the best place in town, but well suited to the executive or professional who needs one more set of good-looking dress clothes. Here is a decent selection of top-quality designers at about 50 percent off. Suits can be found in cashmere, wool, and camel's hair. At last look, a specially crafted Burberry trench coat with wool lining was selling for $225.

See coupon in the back.

VICTORY SHIRT COMPANY
485 Madison Avenue
753-1679
American Express, MC, Visa

This store is owned by the manufacturer of Brooks Brothers shirts, so already you know they are going to be a bargain. They sell a wide range of dress shirts, and the owner calls the stock "preppy and not casual office wear." They offer hand-monogramming and custom tapering. Their special monthly sales are thematic, just to keep things interesting. One recent month they took 20 percent off all blue shirts, the next month they offered 20 percent off on all stripes.

Having moved into a larger space, Victory has been able to order more stock and thus make the prices even lower. You are going to get any shirt here at 25 percent less than you would at department stores. This is another good chance to buy from the source; don't wait until you have to purchase it on the shelves.

HATS!

From **J.J. Hat Shop** (1276 Broadway, 502-5012; American Express, MC, Visa; closed Sunday) to downtown's supreme old hat shop **Young's Hats** (193 Nassau Street, 964-5693; American Express, MC, Visa; closed Sunday), you can find great discounts on ancient and new-fangled head-toppers. At J.J.'s, they sell the foreign brands and styles, such as Panama hats, Valare's, and even French and fisherman for under $15. J.J. can fit any head. They also have many bolo ties, starting at $10 and going up to

$100. Young's is more traditional, with only sizes 6 5/8 – 7 3/4. They have a fine selection of cowboy and opera hats—and Stetsons, too—but nothing of the wild and trendy "Indy Jones" or "Dick Tracy" caps that J.J. excels in.

Hat lovers should hop on over to **Modern Hatters** (313 Third Street, Jersey City, New Jersey, 201/659-1113; checks accepted), where this family business offers all name-brand hats for both sexes at 40 percent less than most Manhattan stores. For $35, they will even order you a custom-designed Western hat. This is a loss-leader to get you to come out and see them. And the stock is worth traveling for!

For more menswear, see chapter 3, "Sample Sales."

CHAPTER 13

Womenswear

Women dominate this book. Take a look at the pages of this chapter, and throughout the book, and you will note that women's clothing and accessories can be found in nearly every section. That's because New Jersey, upstate New York, the mail, Orchard Street, shoe stores, sample sales, outerwear places, and even many of the men's clothing stores all feature bargains on women's clothing.

This chapter is dedicated to special stores, none of which fall under any specific umbrella. (See the section titled "Umbrellas," however, in chapter 17, "Stationery and Household Items.") Once you find a store you fully appreciate, remember to be faithful to it. In this area of high rents and heavy competition, stores can go under quickly.

PANDEMONIUM
2133 Broadway
874-9342
American Express, MC, Visa

You can find anything in colorful clothing at Pandemonium, ranging in price from $15 to $50. Included are
tie-dyed shirts, good-looking "T's," brightly colored jackets, vests, pants, shorts, and swimsuits. Look for simple
tank tops at $8 and, when in season, heavier winter wear,
starting at $10. I recommend you visit at the beginning of
the spring when Pandemonium gets the pastel urge, opens
the windows, puts stock on the sidewalk for display, and
lowers its prices. Brands include French Connection, the
Pandemonium brand, and better-name T-shirts and sweats
by Kiss and Jargon. Mix-and-match couture is the name
of the game at this upper west side bargain outlet. (See
Unique Clothing Wearhouse below for a downtown selection of the clothing made by Pandemonium.)

Antique Boutique (712 and 714 Broadway, 227 East
59th Street, 460-8830; American Express, MC, Visa) has
more expensive variations of the wares found here. And
the woman's department of **Canal Jeans** (504 Broadway,
226-1140; American Express, MC, Visa) (see chapter 12,
"Menswear") has a larger selection of casual clothing,
though Pandemonium's prices are still better.

DAMAGES
768 Madison Avenue and several stores by the same
name on Warren, Murray, and Chambers Streets
535-9030
Uptown store accepts American Express, MC, Visa

You get the idea that everything in here is a little less
than perfect. For instance, when you see a sweater or a
skirt at a price lower than what you could have expected
five years ago, you have to be suspicious. When pressed,
the sales clerks will tell you there's a thread missing or
something amiss with the label.

It doesn't matter, though. You can get any Italian, French, or domestic designer's material, many of which are samples from the stock of their collections, and you'll be very happy.

The Warren, Murray, and Chambers Street stores are a variation on the theme: everything is stacked in bins and costs less than $10. On Warren, you'll find underwear, silks, and blouses, in addition to surprises shipped in daily. Nobody will know you bought the item at a "Damages." Except maybe your banker.

AARON'S
627 Fifth Avenue, Brooklyn, take "R" to
Prospect Avenue
718/768-5400
American Express, MC, Visa

There's an old saying: If you don't know someone in the clothing business, you'd better shop carefully. Get thee to Aaron's, where there is more discount designer clothing under one roof than anywhere in New York. Recently expanded, Aaron's is a crowded warehousey store overflowing with women's bargains at small prices.

Look at the roughly written signs all over the place and you'll be shocked by the many top designers who supply directly to Aaron's. During a recent conversation with a manager, he asked me not to mention the designers' names because he didn't want them to pull out their stock. I must point out Aaron's oft-used slogan: "Serious shopping." And just how serious are they? One Saturday before Christmas I spotted a sign: "No Kids Please."

MS., MISS, OR MRS.
(ALSO KNOWN AS BEN FARBER'S)
462 Seventh Avenue, 3rd Floor
736-0557
Closed Sunday and often Saturday

Some 400 of the top designers converge on this large

are sold at discounts that range from 10 to 60
his recommended stop may be New York's only
.... up" place for women's high fashion: Come here
for tweeds, dresses—evening and casual wear—and a fine
assortment of shirts, tops, sweaters, and hats.

It's not a store to go to for any specific brand-name
item, because you probably won't find it. You will, however, run away with things you didn't know you needed.
Although not packed as full of clothing, another place
duly worth a trip is **Abe Geller** (499 Seventh Avenue, 5th
Floor; American Express, MC, Visa; closed Sunday and
at 3 p.m. on Saturday). Here you might find as much as
70 percent cut off the prices on racks and shelves of top
designer fashions. It depends on what season they were
introduced (the further past, the better the price). Aesthetically, this is a prettier place to shop than Farber's;
pricewise, Geller's is not quite as good a deal.

PARENT PENDING
1178 Lexington Avenue, 988-3996
2007 Broadway, 769-2232
American Express, MC, Visa

If kids are on deck, you'll want to know about the
foremost maternity dressers in town. Gentlemen must
make appointments (it's understandable, if a little preju-
dicial); however, women are always welcome. The prices
are average but the selection is stupendous: from inexpensive smocks and flowery shirts (large sizes only, $40–$60)
to special party outfits and mother-oriented gifts.

WHITTAL & SHON
247 West 37th Street, 9th Floor
Call 718/361-5580 for information about sale dates
MC, Visa

These sales representatives for designers sell women's

clothing, hats, furs, and hair accessories for prices below wholesale. Showroom is open to the public once a month. See coupon in the back.

It's a trendy place that doesn't try to be "in." I was impressed with the number of necessities thrown in with the fashions: nursing bras, instructional manuals and videos, and future father toys.

The only other well-stocked *and* inexpensive maternity store in New York is **Reborn Maternity** (1449 Third Avenue, 737-8817; 565 Columbus Avenue, 362-6965; American Express, MC, Visa; outlets in Queens, Long Island, New Jersey, and Connecticut.) They are always having sales. Regular prices are only so-so, but when discounted, prices on corduroy jumpers, silk dresses, nursing lingerie, pants, and blazers are exceptional. Call to find out dates of seasonal sales.

See chapter 5, "Shop-by-Mail," for **Maternity Warehouse Outlet.**

UNIQUE CLOTHING WAREHOUSE
726 Broadway
674-1863
American Express, MC, Visa

This started in the early 1970s as a small and unusual craftsy clothing store. It has branched out so far that there is now a highly touted Unique label. The store has all women's fashions *and* a gimmicky costume jewelry section that bests the stock of most downtown outlets. I am consistently pleased with the selection of accessories for women, from head bands to brooches to cosmetics and trendy-slogan pins, and just about any belt you could dream of.

This is the shopping center for New York University students—Unique is located for all practical purposes on the N.Y.U. campus. Which explains why you can get any look you want here, and some of it even at wholesale prices. But they are also very good at being "on target," so you can rest assured that whatever you buy here, be it baggy or tight, lustily colorful or black and fashionable, it is certainly *au courant*. The most popular gimmick is Artwear—paintings or color photos transposed onto jackets, T-shirts, and underwear, starting at $10 and done while you wait.

Half the warehouse is for new clothes; the other half is for refurbished bargains: jackets, shirts, pants, and a host of "trashy" surprises such as overalls, flak jackets, and wetsuits! This is also the only place in New York where you can find discounts on the clothing made at the store **Reminiscence** (175 MacDougal Street; 74 Fifth Avenue; Avenue B & Seventh Street; 541-9480; American Express, MC, Visa).

For a unique "trashy" clothing store, turn to **Trash and Vaudeville** (4 St. Marks Place, 982-3590; American Express, MC, Visa), still the original, found on the block where Bohemia began.

THRIFT MARTS

♦ **St. Luke's Thrift Shop** (487 Hudson Street, 924-9364) sells anything the neighborhood residents wish to donate. The clothing is mostly antique or Bohemian and goes for $5–$20, with some dresses selling for $50. For the record, St. Luke's sells other merchandise, such as knickknacks, books and magazines, wine glasss and decanters, brandy snifters, and surprisingly fine household goods. All the money goes into charitable pockets.

♦ **Trishop Thrift Boutique** (1689 First Avenue, 369-2410) is filled with good clothing, including sweaters, blouses, and silk and polyester dresses, with the brand names Evan Picone, Kasper, David Warren,

Liz Claiborne, and more. Prices are way below wholesale and all proceeds go to the Mental Health Association of New York and Bronx.

♦ **Cancer Care Thrift Shop** (1480 Third Avenue, 879-9868) has everything piled up on the shelves. Great shoes, gowns, mini-skirts, and even fine furniture (not sets but individual pieces) can be purchased on any given day. There's a neat grouping of separates, too, such as blazers and skirts that sell for $15–$25. Cancer Care raises money to provide psychological and financial assistance for cancer patients and their families.

♦ **Encore-Resale Dress Shop** (1132 Madison Avenue, 879-2850) is an uncanny place where you'll find hand-me-downs of the rich and famous who live on the upper east side. The owner likes to tell the story of the time Jackie Onassis brought her old gowns in to sell. It's a fancy store, but the prices can be nice. I saw what had to be Cinderella's old-fashioned ball dress here—for $35! It was dusty.

♦ **One Night Stand** (905 Madison Avenue, 772-7720; American Express, MC, Visa) is for those who are in the market for a gown, but only for a little while. Rent elegant dresses from leading designers. And see coupon in the back.

♦ **I, Michael** (1041 Madison Avenue, 2nd Floor; American Express, MC, Visa) is a place for some four thousand gowns sold to this shop's trusted owner by the neighborhood's wealthiest women. There is also a little-known selection of good jackets available at a fraction of their cost new. This store is rarely jam-packed, either. (See chapter 11, "Outerwear.")

S & W LADIES WEAR
165 West 26th Street for sportswear
169 West 26th Street for furs
173 West 26th Street—outlet store
283 Seventh Avenue for shoes
287 Seventh Avenue for outerwear
924-6656
American Express, MC, Visa

Here are current designer women's fashions at a discount of about 25–50 percent in several stores located near each other. S & W is disorganized—you have to scramble to find what you want—but it's worth it, particularly when they hold unadvertised sales. (Call about monthly specials.) Keep in mind that they also place small advertisements in many local newspapers and magazines, and those offer an additional 15–20 percent off sale prices ("with this coupon").

Though S & W's management calls their part of Seventh Avenue "The Stretch," I believe that's stretching a good thing. Only the shop at 173 West 26th Street is a true bargain, although the coat store does have surprises.

For an even greater discount incentive, see coupon in the back.

DAFFY DAN'S
111 Fifth Avenue, 529-4477
335 Madison Avenue, 557-4422
American Express, MC, Visa

Daffy Dan's is a favorite of many New York shoppers. It's probably because this giant store—called "Daffy's" in the suburbs, where the stores are even larger—has a lower level bargain "basement" where last year's models are sold at proper discounts! Let's take a quick look at the Fifth Avenue branch: Thirty-five thousand square feet of clothing with a second floor for current women's fashions and fair prices on skirts, ancient hats, fine sweaters that are rarely discounted, and a selling floor that changes constantly.

If you spend time on Daffy Dan's main floor, be sure to see new designs of costume jewelry, usually at half off. Keep in mind that Daffy's stretches the fashion seasons so that Winter collections are thankfully still being sold well into winter. (See Introduction for explanation of the seasons.) Sure, bargains are to be found here, but you will have to look in the crevices of the bins and racks of this place, which announces "Clothing Bargains for Millionaires."

While we're on the subject of suburban-based bargains, please be sure to visit **Loehmann's** (5740 Broadway, Riverdale, Bronx, 543-6420; take "1" to West 238th Street; American Express, MC, Visa). Most every woman who ventures outside of Manhattan shops at a Loehmann's, which are all located in large spaces with adjacent parking lots. Walk in and encounter dresses, skirts, sweaters, and lingerie, not to mention complete outfits and a host of accessories, all at 30 percent less than regular retail.

CAPEZIO
755 Seventh Avenue and 131 East 61st Street
245-2130
American Express, MC, Visa
Closed Sunday

The worldwide store Capezio is famous for dancewear; it's the largest dance-theater clothing retailer in the world. Last year it branched out to a new location on Seventh Avenue—the one that seems to be the best-stocked.

The location has kiosks and moving mirrors; it's a flashy place to shop. Everywhere you look are tights, fancy dance outfits, shoes, leotards, unitards, swimwear, and nylon and cotton hosiery. There are also 15 distinct dance

eeved and sleeveless dancewear, and all of this at
s that are comparable to other dancewear shops (see
ow). Closeout sales occur nearly every month. Leotards
an $15–$20 and at sale time are priced as low as $5;
ballet slippers drop to $20; tap shoes shimmy down to
$18; canvas shoes are as low as $15.

Hint: They mark down much of their existing shoe
stock during the third week of April, International Dance
Week. Management has, incidentally, added instructional
and entertaining videos at Seventh Avenue, for patrons to
watch while waiting for the interminably slow elevators.

While we're on dancewear and tights, find Danskin
brand at the inexpensive **Barbara Gee Dancewear** (2282
1/2 Broadway and 2487 Broadway, 769-2923; American
Express, MC, Visa; closed Sunday). Barbara Gee has a
good selection of tights, leotards, and dancewear and
while not as renowned or innovative as Capezio, they usually beat them in price. The specialties here are lingerie
and all-cotton underthings made by Danskin, Lily of
France, Maidenform, and Bali.

J. CREW CATALOGUE
One Ivy Crescent, Lynchburg, VA 24506
800/562-0258

My favorite mail-order catalogue is J. Crew's. See
chapter 5, "Shop-by-Mail." They continually surprise
shoppers with women's front-tees ($15) and the famous
Crew line of rugged rugby shirts and sweaters ($38). Also
find knit shirts, socks, hats, and a full line of winter, fall,
and spring jackets, including one jean jacket with "that
broken-in look" ($52).

Call their special service number (800/782-8244) to
have a catalogue whisked to you in a matter of days.
Unlike many companies, J. Crew seems anxious to please
and even understands your trepidation about shopping
through the mail. They make it simple by confirming ex-

actly what you're getting, checking the order twice by phone, and then regularly sending fliers announcing clearance sales by mail! They have been in business for decades; they strive to be your first choice in activewear.

They have a New York store that features many of the same items (but not the same sales) as the mail-order catalogue: South Street Seaport, 203 Front Street, 385-3500; American Express, MC, Visa.

For more womenswear, see chapter 3, "Sample Sales."

CHAPTER 14

Children's Wear

Children can wear a great deal of clothes, and wear them out fast. So it's important to shop where bargains are to be had year round, and where the selections are good. Right now, with all the kids' places popping up throughout the five boroughs I've noticed a trend toward expensive, boutiquey clothes that look great in the store, but cost too much and can be gotten cheaper.

ONCE UPON A TIME
171 East 92nd Street
831-7619
MC, Visa
Closed Sunday

Starting with the smallest kids and moving up to finicky teens, Once Upon a Time sells secondhand items that, depending on when you visit, range in price from 20 to

50 percent less than retail. Besides, the owners boast a full range of seasonal clothing for people who don't want to buy their kids' bathing suits in winter.

MOUSE 'N AROUND
197 Bleecker Street; 529-5656;
1274 Lexington Avenue, 289-1554
American Express, checks

This is a Mickey Mouse dynasty, not at all like Disney shops in smalltown malls. This is more of a place where the "coolest" Mickey and Minnie paraphernalia can be found. Whenever they have a sale, and that's pretty often, prices are dropped by 40 percent for all their cartoonish sweatshirts, "T's," and other activewear.

I enjoy the Garbage Pail kids clothing, which retails for under $30 here, and is virtually impossible to buy anywhere else. Mickey hardcores can find acrylic sweaters in all Mouse sizes, selling for under $30 at regular price, emblazoned with Mickey and the other Disney cartoon characters. The big sales take place when the various Disney and Looney Tunes merchandisers become overstocked. Call for details.

WENDY'S STORE
1046 Madison Avenue
MC, Visa
Closed Sunday

Oh, I love Wendy Worth. She sells tiny-sized everythings. For instance, you can find vests, booties, sweaters, hand-painted T-shirts, Peter Rabbit and Babar quilts, overalls, and Scrabble necklaces. It's a fashion wonderland with prices that will surprise you and, as in all good uptown boutiques, racks way in the back where closeouts and specials are displayed regularly. Also find cowboy boots—little ones—and some jewelry. Prices start at a few dollars for socks and puffy-sleeved "T's," and run above $100 for that perfect party dress.

MEXX
1410 Broadway, 2nd Floor
764-5890

Open to the public on special sale dates only.

While we're on fashionable subjects, I know of one special manufacturer that opens up twice a year for sales on new children's merchandise: fine dresses, jackets, blazers, skirts, sweaters, pants, and even pantsuits for little girls and boys—and men and women, too. Mexx is the sale to head to at the end of December and again in June when they open up their warehouse to the public for extraordinary clothing values that are worth stopping up for. Call at the beginning of those months and then, forward march!

AIDA'S AND JIMI'S MERCHANDISING COMPANY
41 West 28th Street, 2nd Floor
689-2415
American Express, MC, Visa
Closed Sunday (open Saturday by appointment)

This outlet has girls' dresses found in better department stores. Sizes infant to 14 are constantly closed out here in special sales. Best advice: go to the store at the beginning of the month, when all new merchandise comes in. Then wander through the old items—they're not very old. Sale prices for casual and dress shoes start at $14 while regular prices on dresses for little girls are $12–$60.

See coupon in the back for further savings. See chapter 3, "Sample Sales."

RICE & BRESKIN
325 Grand Street
925-5515
MC, Visa
Closed Saturday (and early Friday)

Everything at Rice & Breskin is sold at 20 percent less than you'd find elsewhere. This has been the shop to go to for fifty years for fine-name merchandise with sizes up to 14. Everything here is wrapped in plastic like a sofa slipcover: a snowsuit costs $30, a blouse goes for $7, a beret costs $5. I was told I'd be hard-pressed to find something over $40, but I did catch a boy's suit jacket for $45. The salesperson heard me telling the "over $40" story and lowered the price to $39. Go figure.

S. KLEIN KIDDIE SHOP
155 Orchard Street
475-9470
American Express, MC, Visa

A baby will be well equipped whose guardian shops at S. Klein, one of the oldest kids' stores in Manhattan. Hardly anything for little people is above $15, and that includes comforter sets, layette sets, pajamas, and party dresses. They claim that about 30 percent of all their stock is "irregular" merchandise. That's good news for you: that slight defect—a thread is loose or the color ran a drop—means you get it at 70 percent off!

NATHAN BORLAM
157 Havemeyer Street, Brooklyn
Take the "J/M" to Marcy Avenue
718/782-0108
Checks accepted
Closed Saturday

A stereotypically Brooklyn Jewish shop; that means

bargains galore! Here are brand-name clothes for boys and girls at half of what they are in department stores. (And they *are* found in department stores' current stock!) Featured are nationally known brands, imported and designer clothes. Nathan has tights, jeans, bathing suits, dresses—most anything you'd expect in an uptown children's store. It's just that Nathan's is more crowded!

SECOND ACT
1046 Madison Avenue
988-2440
Closed Sunday and Monday

Leave them in the play area for kids that you find when you walk in, and walk around browsing for toys, books, some furniture, and clothes sizes infant to 16. Everything is hand-me-down, but in most cases you would never know it. Prices start at $1.

ROBIN'S NEST
1397 Second Avenue
737-2004
American Express, MC, Visa
Closed Sunday

The ultimate in winter and summer specialists: a store that looks expensive, almost daunting, from the outside. But then you walk in and, presto! you've discovered another world. From corduroy shirts and pants—boys' and girls', all sizes—to coats, snowsuits, and sportjackets, everything is at unbelievably good uptown prices. I even found imported sneakers for $16! Surprise, surprise. Don't forget flannel, velvet, and leather skirts and dresses for girls, starting at $27. It's a dream come true for children's clothing buyers who can't find anything affordable.

THE GAP FOR KIDS
2373 Broadway, 873-2044; 91 Seventh Avenue, 989-0195; 527 Madison Avenue, 688-1260; 1164 Madison Avenue, 517-5202; 250 West 57th Street, 956-3140; 354 Avenue of Americas, 777-2420; 215 Columbus Avenue, 874-3740; Gap Outlet (kids sale items) 643-8960 and 695-2521, 34th and Sixth Also: Baby Gaps for the littlest fashion victim to be found at 250 West 57th Street, 1164 Madison Avenue and 354 Sixth Avenue. Gaps in the boroughs, New York state, Long Island, New Jersey, and Connecticut
American Express, MC, Visa

A good children's "hip clothing" store, with some surprising bargains for all ages. After The Gap repositioned itself as a not-just-Levi's boutique, I was shocked to find they sold kid's denim jackets for under $30. The new Gap hawks small versions of everything they sell for adults—only the values are better for wee ones. Try $8–$10 T-shirts, $15 colorful shorts, $5 visors and sunglasses, and a host of $10–$50 outerwear (coats, jackets, rainwear), created with tiny styles in mind.

For more bargains in children's wear, see chapter 5, "Shop-by-Mail," and chapter 3, "Sample Sales."

CHAPTER 15

Cosmetics
and Perfumes

Here's a chapter to help you get the maximum from the area's most unique cosmetic and perfume discounters. While you're at it you may want to get in better shape all around. What I discuss here is everything designed to make you look good.

CATALOGUES FOR A BEAUTIFUL YOU

Buy from wholesalers as much as possible. For instance, **Beautiful Visions USA LTD** (516/576-9000) is a well-known way to buy cosmetics. They boast that the cosmetic products in their giant free catalogue are 75 percent less than regular prices: products by Max Factor, Elizabeth Arden, Helena Rubinstein, and most current manufacturers. I read "75 percent," but based on a comparison with Manhattan stores, their prices reach to discounts as high as *90 percent off!*

The **Beauty Showcase** is another place to try, but only through the mail (write 714 Sunset Boulevard, Beverly Hills, CA 90215, no phone). Everything you might want is here at a fraction below wholesale outlet costs. Beauty products include the names Dana, Le Galion, Frances Denney, Anne Klein, and Polly Bergen. Their catalogue offers "special gifts and bonuses" for return shoppers. That mystery is worth writing in for. See chapter 5, "Shop-by-Mail."

PERFUME DISTRICT

Perfumes are in plentiful supply in New York's small perfume district (see chapter 2, "Comprehending the Districts"), on 17th Street between Broadway and Sixth Avenue. The best to shop in are **Jerry's Job Lot** (#9), a messy store with good perfume prices but a limited selection—they have sample bottles for $2, and a fine selection of cachets for less than $5; and **Jay's Perfume Bar** (#28), which features gigantic daily specials. The famed **Perfume Encounter** (#25) might be a better bet, with French scents *and* a free gift for purchasing anything in stock. Several neighboring shops say "Wholesale Only" on doors and windows, but you can still go in and talk prices, albeit quietly. The best bargains on 17th Street are small sample bottles of cologne normally given out if you are a good customer uptown at Van Cleef & Arpels' counter. These are sold on 17th Street for $2.

Around the corner, upstairs at **Parisian Perfumes** (123 Fifth Avenue, 2nd floor, 254-5300; American Express, MC, Visa; closed Sunday) find some of the best off-price selections—not Cher's or Elizabeth Taylor's. In a noisy store with a radio or television always playing you will note small Chanel bottles, and 2.5-ounce samples of body lotions and oil versions of colognes "pour homme" for 60 percent less than other scent-sational stores.

Find Passion, Krystle, Nina Ricci, and even more at Parisian. A great gift idea is the Coty and Halston perfume-and-more packs for $20, $35, and $79 featuring soap, perfume, aftershaves and lotions in a beautifully arranged kit.

Along nearby West 14th Street, look into the small stalls in between the stores that are right on the sidewalk. There are good, dependable savings on bottles of the latest perfumes. But do make sure the bottle is wrapped tightly, or you might be getting a partially filled or watered-down one.

V & Q HEALTH AND BEAUTY
666 Fifth Avenue, in the subway arcade
Closed Sunday

It's an odd place to shop, but if you are collector of cosmetics, notably Maybelline, Max Factor, and the Revlon collection of eyeliners, you should enter the underground arcade from 54th Street (next to B. Dalton Books). Also find small costume jewelry and an odd assortment of health and weight-loss drinks. In winter they have a large Lancôme stock.

EXOTIC FRAGRANCES
1490 Lexington Avenue
410-0600
Closed Sunday

This uptown store is an Eastern delight: fine imported Asian perfumes and scents (oils, herbs, and potions) at wholesale prices. They boast 100 scents, and even some remakes of the famous fragrances at half the price. Here are a great many bottled odors you will not find elsewhere in New York.

JEAN-PIERRE SAND SKIN CARE
P.O. Box 263, Riverdale, NY 10471
No phone
MC, Visa

Many French perfumes and skin care lotions can be ordered through the mail. Everything you might wish from a smell or a lotion is available here at a very low price. When asked how, the owners point out, "These fragrances have only been trademarked, not patented. We merely duplicate the fragrances." Thus a bottle of Joy that sells for $41 an ounce at Sak's is broken down to cost $12.95, which includes $1 for the packaging, 3¢ for the alcohol, $4 for the bottle itself, $1 for the labor, $2 for the perfume "essence." Sounds fair, right?

Delivery is free; for quick second day delivery, add five percent to the tab. See coupon in the back.

ESSENTIAL PRODUCTS
90 Water Street
344-4288
Closed Saturday and Sunday

This establishment offers elegant versions of famed scents, just like the Jean-Pierre folks do. However, Essential's prices are unbeatable. They stock over sixty copies of Coco, Eternity, Giorgio, Joy, L'Air, and Zazanie (a popular men's choice). You can order a one-ounce perfume for around $20—either through the mail by check or money order, or at the counter. You can also ask for sample cards, which is a little like going into an ice cream parlor and requesting "a taste."

Essential has been a fly in the ointment for the prestigious perfume firms for nearly a century. While consumers love them, perfumeries would love to see them out of business. See coupon in the back.

SWISS SUN TANNING SALON
**50 West 22nd Street; 220 East 23rd Street;
1229 Second Avenue; 53 Greenwich Avenue
679-7100
American Express, MC, Visa**

This is a safer tanning salon because they use a special machine from Switzerland that gives out beta rays less harsh than the radiation from American-made machines. Swiss Sun can be a bargain, too, if you buy a quantity of sessions. See coupon in the back.

EXCLUSIVELY YOURS PERSONAL TRAINERS
**244 Front Street, 1st Floor
571-6315
Closed Saturday and Sunday**

Personal trainers for exercise are expensive, right? See coupon in the back and go to this place where you can get an unbeatable deal of five workouts with a specialist—including Nautilus and free weights—for just $99.

While we're on the subject of toning up, how about a relatively inexpensive workout at **Competitive Edge Fitness** (151 West 19th Street, 691-1166; MC, Visa) where sweating is on sale and where they offer free try-outs for new customers.

CHRISTINE VALMY SCHOOL
**260 Fifth Avenue
581-1520
Closed Sunday**

You can get a $15 facial here; quality is stupendous.

CHEAP HAIRCUTTERS

♦ The best cheap cuts in town for men and women—and the most entertaining—are at **Astor Place** (2 Astor Place, 529-5761). No reservations, just a $10 cut by an assembly line of cutters. You can dance there, because the music is always on, and people seem to be constantly in a good mood. See the coupon in the back.

♦ **Frank's** (303B Columbus Avenue, no phone number; closed Sunday) is a small shop where you can get a cut, but no hair gel.

♦ **Berkeley's** (287B Amsterdam, no phone; closed Sunday) is a small house, too. The old-fashioned shaves there are a pampered man's best friend!

♦ **Wavelengths** (60 East 42nd Street, 697-4283; closed Sunday) has a $25 women's and $20 men's special.

♦ **Shortcuts for Kids** (104 West 83rd Street, 877-2277; closed Sunday) is a bargain with very cheap cuts for kids and a fun atmosphere. See coupon in the back.

♦ **Norbert Hairstylists,** near New York University (16 East Eighth Street, 473-1330) offers student cuts for $12.50 and manicures for $6. See coupon in the back.

♦ A nice price for adult hair care is found at **Picasso Hairstylists** (150 Fifth Avenue, 206-9004; closed Sunday). Their slogan runs: "A new you for a very small fee." See coupon in the back.

FREEBIE HAIRCUTTERS AND MORE

In many cases salons offer free haircuts when they are trying to re-train or qualify their cutters. Many times the barber will have final say in how your hair should be styled. Don't worry, because the beauticians want you to look your best and would not want to try something *too* bold.

◆ At **Vidal Sassoon** (767 Fifth Avenue, 535-9200) you can get a free shampoo, cut, and blow dry on specific evenings every week.

◆ Since **Glemby International** (116 East 16th Street, 979-3000) staffs styling booths all over the nation, they need heads of hair on which to perfect their skills. The trainees have just graduated school and this, in effect, is their "internship." Call for information on very specific hours.

◆ **John Atchison** (44 West 55th Street, 265-6870) cuts hair for a few clients a week. You tell the stylist what to do.

◆ **Clairol Test Center** (345 Park Avenue, 546-2715) offers complimentary beauty services to evaluate new products. Again, don't worry, because everything they test has received FDA approval. They are mainly looking for labeling specifications. Call for an appointment five days a week.

◆ **Clairol Consumer Research Center** (345 Park Avenue, 546-2707) has products you take home in order to return with results.

◆ **L'Oreal Beauty Response Center** (Fifth Avenue and 47th Street, 984-4164) offers tests on certain products weekly. A bonus is that they give you a gift package just for the testing!

◆ **Revlon Professional Products** (555 West 57th Street, 15th Floor, 408-8085) tests haircare products like perms, haircolor, and relaxing techniques in what they call their "evaluation center."

STOCKING UP: THE TRICK

◆ A Place like **A to Z Discounts** (239 West 14th Street, 691-3930) will be of help when you want to pur-

chase all the goods you need at one time.
they're not related, there's an uptown stockir
place, too, named **A to Z** (930 Second Avenue, 9
6464; American Express, MC, Visa).

- **Lo-Price Discount** (323 Eighth Avenue; American
  Express, MC, Visa) has prices low enough for you
  to find stock for your bathrooms so you need not
  visit a drug store very often.

- The best place to find sample bottles is at **Price Wise,
  Inc.** (2121 Broadway; 2234 Broadway; and 336 East
  86th Street; 595-6540; American Express, MC,
  Visa). Price Wise has every little bottle for your hair,
  skin, and even eyes, including spritz bottles to keep
  the hair stiff, lotions for sore eyes and contact lenses,
  and even shampoos and conditioners by L'Oreal.
  Professional care liquids include Neutrogena ($1.49)
  and Extra Strength Keri Lotion for dry skin ($.99).
  They carry Intensive Care lotion in tiny bottles for
  just $.89, and a variety of soft soaps.

- An entire line of sample products by Vidal Sassoon
  is on the shelves at **Ricky's,** a new chain all over
  downtown and moving further uptown soon (for
  chain locations call 924-3401; American Express,
  MC, Visa). You may be suspicious as to why Vidal
  Sassoon would sell a small bottle of finishing rinse
  for $.50. Actually, it's good for business. These are
  incentive items that Sassoon and others give stores
  as a friendly gesture. The stores sell them for $.50
  to customers who put them in travel kits or try out
  a new product. And then *everyone* looks good.

- **McKay Drugs** (253 First Avenue; 55 Fifth Avenue;
  307 Sixth Avenue; 627-2300; American Express,
  MC, Visa) has daily closeouts, unadvertised specials,
  and managers with vivid imaginations who will
  stock newfangled products when available. See coupon in the back. McKay has nearly every perfume at

e with upscale places such as **Cos-**
low).

)f an endangered species in New
)harmacy: a place you can find
)ur prescription filled at a rea-
ꞁast few years, expensive private
ꞁave opened up and started charging outland-
ꞁn prices for all prescriptions. It is only when you price
around you realize you *can* do better.

For more on "stocking up," see Introduction.

COSMETICS PLUS
275 Seventh Avenue; 518 Fifth Avenue; 515 Madison
Avenue; 1203 Third Avenue
924-3493
American Express, MC, Visa

This large and pretty series of stores calls itself the
"American parfumerie," and it is, indeed, the best perfume
chain outlet going. While tags on regular drug store stock
like aspirin and Band-Aids are only so-so, the perfume
and cologne selections, and the helpful people who work
at Cosmetics Plus, are superior; and the atmosphere lends
itself to purchasing hair and body products.

Theirs is an odd assortment of bathroom appliances
(hair dryers, Water Piks, electric toothbrushes, curlers,
etc.). You will find nice pickings in sample bottles, including plenty of different sprays, hair gels, and conditioners
(Neutrogena, Head and Shoulders, Vidal Sassoon), and a
buy-three-get-one-free Hanes pantyhose offer.

Be sure to look into their extensive collection of Paul
Mitchell and L'Oreal products at market prices. Selection
is key at the low-key Cosmetics Plus.

For discounts on Clinique products, call **The Beauty**
Boutique (216/826-3008) in Cleveland.

THE BODY SHOP
**747 Broadway; 2159 Broadway; 901 Sixth Avenue
(inside A & S Plaza); 773 Lexington Avenue;
485 Madison Avenue; 16 Fulton Street
800/541-2535 for a catalogue or information**

All over the world people visit the Body Shop, which originated in West Sussex, England. It's not for their prices. Body Shop is *not* cheap for hair and body products, but they "act globally," meaning the products are non-exploitative, or politically correct: They use vegetable instead of animal ingredients in their products; they offer a recycling discount to customers who bring back the biodegradable bottles, jars, and tubes; ingredients are "close-to-source"; and they do not use elaborate packaging.

If you shop for natural products at another boutique that also manufacturers its own—namely **Kiehls** (109 Third Avenue, 475-3400; American Express, MC, Visa)—you will find they have the same types of natural goods, but they are more expensive than Body Shop. (Kiehls has good closeout sales, so get on their mailing list.)

MR. M'S
**192 Seventh Avenue South
741-2225
American Express, Visa**

The natural products of the health-conscious company "Tom's of Maine" are sold at a discount at Mr. M's. This discounter also sells a great variety of other natural goods—toothpastes, mouthwashes, rinses, and has great prices on such basics as toilet paper, shampoo, conditioners, health products, and other bathroom necessities. I should mention that Mr. M's is an elite supplier of "samplers," which are small bottles of shampoo, conditioner, mouthwash, ointments, and assorted goodies, sold at under a dollar as a promotion.

CHAPTER 16

Jewelry Ideas

Unlike European cities, New York is filled with inexpensive places to buy jewelry. This chapter is about the many good buys found in the New York area; mostly it's filled with some of the more imaginative places to buy wearable jewels. You can, if you wish, visit the more expensive jewelry emporiums which often cut their prices, though inexplicably: **Tiffany & Company** (727 Fifth Avenue, 755-8000) has a third floor filled with exquisite knickknacks that can often cost only $50; **Cartier** (2 East 52nd Street, 753-0111; Madison Avenue & 70th Street, 249-3240; 725 Fifth Avenue, 308-0840) is a watch and fine trinket manufacturer extraordinaire; and **Fortunoff's** (681 Fifth Avenue, 758-6660) is best described as a discount *and* costly fine jewelry department store. (All major credit cards are accepted at all locations.)

For a diamond purchase at bargain prices, visit West 47th Street between Fifth and Sixth Avenues, Manhattan's so-called "Jewelry District." (See Rennie Ellen—whose service is so busy she has been dubbed "Mayor of 47th Street"—below.) 578 Fifth Avenue at West 47th Street is the **International Jewelry Mart,** the United States' premier place to purchase diamonds, and a very upscale market. 4 West 47th Street is the **National Jewelry Mart,** where you can buy folksy pieces.

For information on West 47th Street, see chapter 2, "Comprehending the Districts." Jewelry is also found in chapter 5, "Shop-by-Mail," chapter 13, "Womenswear," and chapter 4, "Flea Markets."

ADRIENNE JEWELRY SPECIALISTS
52 West 47th Street
869-3230
American Express, MC, Visa

Adrienne is a gem of a sales lady who makes house and office calls only. Unlike many of her colleagues, Adrienne believes in dropping prices regularly. She makes her own gold designs and creates copies that are indistinguishable from the originals. Rings, earrings, and bracelets are made to order. Adrienne will also negotiate.

See coupon in the back.

SHERU ENTERPRISES
49 West 38th Street
730-0766
American Express, MC, Visa
Closed Sunday

Marcasite, bakelite, rhinestones, Austrian crystals, and semi-precious beads are just the beginning of what this craft supply house sells to the wholesale and retail market. Go here when you're experimenting and don't want to waste money on accessories. Included in their wide stock are metal ornaments, chains, sequins, studs, and all types of appliqués. All sterling silver items are cut a straight 50 percent, and you can get parts like earwires and tiny pins for those intricate—and broken—jewelry pieces.

THE MUSEUM OF FOLK ART GIFT SHOP
62 West 50th Street, 247-5611
2 Lincoln Square, 496-2966
American Express, MC, Visa
Closed Sunday on 50th Street

This is one of the most unlikely places to get great prices on a fabulous assortment of bracelets, earrings, pendants, pins, and other fun jewelry. Everything here is folksy and made by local designers and nationwide artists, and runs $3–$18. They have pewter, brass, and special "urban art" made of copper—a penny bracelet costs $3— all sold under the auspices of the museum. If you like pins in the shapes of tyrannosauruses, dolphins, and cows, you can have a ball at this craft shop.

And since everybody who works here is a volunteer, you'll never get a hard sell.

Be sure to see Michele Stivoletto's teak-and-silver pendants, along with neat brooches from hippie days, and Shaker art. There's no gold here, but certainly tons of silver!

Another museum shop where fantastic folk jewelry is sold is **Whitney Museum of American Art** (945 Madison Avenue, 606-0201); American Express, MC, Visa).

Membership in each of New York's museums usually costs around $30 a year. When you enroll you commonly receive an automatic discount to the gift shops, which makes purchasing jewelry there a snap. Gift shops are found at the Museum of Modern Art, the American Museum of Natural History, the Cooper-Hewitt Museum, the

Jewish Museum, the Indian Museum, and the Metropolitan Museum of Art. Some of these sell fascinating jewelry.

KIRK'S FOLLY
1389 Fifth Avenue, 12th Floor
683-9797

In the course of researching this book I came across several jewelry showrooms that gave special sales every few months; they requested that I not mention the events. (They did not want to be assaulted with phone calls.) But since the manufacturer Kirk's Folly has such great jewelry—and holds such gigantic sales—I must make an exception: Call them and find out when the spring, fall, and winter "stock sales" are being held. When you attend you will encounter 70 percent savings on Kirk's Folly overruns on antique-style earrings, cameo pins, wristwatches (some with rhinestones!), and beautiful hair bows. At the last sale I saw a dressing table and mirror set sold for $45! They may not be cooperative on the phone, but be persistent.

DIAMONDS BY RENNIE ELLEN
15 West 47th Street
869-5525
Checks accepted

The woman I came in contact with at Diamonds by Rennie Ellen would not say if she *was* Rennie or not, but who cares? Her prices on engagement rings are 75 percent below jewelry stores. All shapes and sizes of diamonds are available, and her special artistry is displayed at her small factory in room 401 in the "Diamond Building."

Diamonds By Rennie cautions you to "make appointments well in advance." Returns are accepted within five days, no questions asked. In days of fly-by-night jewelers, that's a relief.

BIANCO'S
409 Bay Ridge Avenue, Brooklyn
Take "R" to Bay Ridge Avenue
(main stop for shopping in that area)
718/748-3020
American Express
Closed Sunday

Many years ago, on my first shopping trip to Brooklyn, I stumbled upon a family-owned operation that sells mostly 18k gold pieces and antique settings. For almost half a century this bunch has handed down the business from generation to generation, along with the understanding that nobody should pay a lot for a piece of jewelry. Prices start at $80 for wholesale-priced estate jewelry and watches that the Bianco family swears are 25 percent below list.

One of them will appraise your stones or old pocket watches and they will probably make you an offer you can't refuse.

WEINSTOCK & YAEGER
23 West 47th Street
819-0413
American Express, MC, Visa
Closed Sunday

You might want to see Weinstock & Yaeger, the best discounter for watches, before you buy any watch: This company promises to beat any deal on both high-end and low-end watches. They boast their wares with a neon announcement: "The Largest Watch Discounter." You will save 40–50 percent on gift watches, too, including gimmicky ones like Swatch and the New York City watch. (Weinstock & Yaeger carries the official watch of every U.S. city.)

Get the name and model number and then call for a quote.

NAPIER COMPANY FACTORY STORE
1231 East Main Street, Meridien, Connecticut
Take the East Main Street exit off I-91
203/238-3087
MC, Visa
Closed Sunday

My jewelry spies tell me that costume buffs should head to Connecticut for the discounts at the Napier Company Factory Store, which carries the well-known Napier costume jewelry found in all department stores and most boutiques on the East Coast. For one hundred years, Napier has been making silver-plated and gold-plated costume pieces with lacquer stones and pearls. Everything at this particular Napier outlet is discounted at 40 percent off the retail price.

The Napier Company Factory Store recently expanded, too, so now they go even further, constantly closing out stock in their line. They are famous for December closeouts, when Christmas means magic for Napier's customers.

Napier celebrates its continual success twice a year with sales in July and October, when the usual 40 percent savings is made even better by a "50 percent off sale," which calculates to 90 percent less than retail! Call to get on their mailing list.

MARCUS & COMPANY APPRAISERS
Empire State Building, 34th Street between Fifth and Sixth Avenues, Suite 1303
736-0808

Sometimes an appraisal can be an intimidating experience. Marcus & Company, in business for decades, will provide you with an experienced hand in figuring the value of your possession. Plus, they give immediate cash payment and require no personal information about your valuables. They will issue appraisal documents for insurance purposes.

DETAIL
383 Lafayette Street
925-8982
Checks accepted

A New York story: For over a decade British-born Anthony Robinson ran a popular store in Soho that sold jewelry of his own design in addition to pieces created by local artists. Although the pieces were expensive, Robinson made sure he had something in store for less than $100. Then his landlord raised the rent so high that Robinson closed the shop and now sells wholesale to department stores and boutiques. That is, *except* when he holds his closeouts, when the public can get their hands on the Detail line at off-price by catalogue, through the mail, and at his showroom.

Detail is now sold at Barney's, Bergdorf's, and other high-end department stores; but you wouldn't know it, because Robinson would rather not put his name on store-bought designs. He sells bracelets, necklaces, earrings, and eccentric jewelry including last year's gorgeous, enormous beetle brooches. Call him and ask for a recent book. Robinson's philosophy is distinctive and his artwear matches that style.

Prices range from $75 to upwards of $1000.

CHAPTER 17

Stationery and Household Items

STAPLES, THE OFFICE SUPERSTORE
1075 Avenue of the Americas
944-6744
MC, Visa
Closed Sunday

For years, the Staples warehouse system of buying stationery goods and merchandise for the home has been a big success in other areas of the country. Recently Staples found a Manhattan space big enough to hold their wares and brought their amazing prices and great system to the tri-state area. It's a simple method: They buy everything in bulk and pass the savings on to you. (Since the success of the Manhattan branch, Staples warehouses have opened in Norwalk and Wilton, Connecticut; Yonkers and Port Chester, New York; and several in New Jersey.)

Staples has the lowest prices you can find on over fifty-five hundred items, including goods for the office, kitchen, bathroom, computer, and even some personal necessities (e.g., a $30 mini-cassette recorder or a $19.99 Texas Instruments battery-operated phone book). You can find "executive swivel chairs" for just $198 (a 47 percent savings), and tiny data cases for 5 1/4″ diskettes sell for $5.99 (a 39 percent savings). By using a free Staples membership card you save an additional 10 percent—just by presenting it at the checkout. This is their way of keeping you on their much-used mailing list.

When you come to the store you will be shocked at the number of loss-leader items they sell to get you there. At last count these included ten boxes of paper clips for $1.39; a box of computer paper for $8.99; fifty diskettes for $27.99—a savings of 71 percent!—and a refill of a daily desk calendar for a mere $9.49. Staples also sells attaché cases, briefcases, portfolios, and small luggage pieces, at between 25 and 50 percent off retail prices. (For more money-saving luggage ideas, see chapter 18, "Luggage and Carry-Alls.")

Staples also delivers for a nominal fee. Need more examples of how great this supermarket of stationery and household items is? How about a 12-pack of 100 watt soft white bulbs ($6.89) or a 48-pack of bathroom tissue ($9.99)? . . .

ROBIN IMPORTERS
510 Madison Avenue
753-6475
American Express, MC, Visa
Closed Sunday (and Saturday in summer only)

They bill themselves as offering "affordable elegance on name-brand table top lines, china, crystal, flatware, and linens," and indeed Robin Importers is one of the best sources for stoneware, flatware, and fine cutlery, with names like Wm. Fraser, Dalia, Supreme, Hachman, Oneida, and Georgian House. They house such brands of china as Thomas, Block, Arzberg, Rosenthal, Fabrik, and Metlox.

In addition, you can find just about anything in housewares here, including ten well-known brands of coffee maker, Copco kitchen storage units, and all sizes of Carefree table linens, which come in twenty-six colors.

GEMINI PAPER GOODS
449 Third Street, Park Slope, Brooklyn
718/768-5568

Here's a place for a great selection of paper goods. You can find a nice gift, promotion, office supply, or party favor through the folks at Gemini. You can get anything you might need in paper goods printed to your specifications *and* at bargain-basement prices: matches, napkins, stirrers, placecards, buttons, menus, and even yarmulkes—all engraved. A typical discount is, for example, preprinted buttons, at $75 per 50 plus $30 for printing. Stripes can be added to each for 16¢. They offer bulk discounts, too. Place your order by phone.

See coupon in the back.

AMAZING FOODS
807 Washington Street
645-4166
Checks accepted
Open to the public Friday

What bargain book would be complete without a peek at food? As I mentioned before, it will save you money to purchase from restaurant suppliers who also sell to the public. Amazing is one of the best of that breed. Three days a week they sell free range chickens ($2.25/lb.); good baby lettuce ($5/half-lb.); Ceylon oysters ($.50 each); Maine scallops ($8.50/lb.); shiitake mushrooms ($6.95/lb.), and Scottish salmon ($18.95/lb.). Don't doubt there is more to be found here, depending on what season you take in Amazing.

KING ARTHUR'S LIQUIDATION CENTER (ARENA LIQUIDATORS)
123 Frost Street, in Westbury, Long Island
516/333-8840
MC, Visa

Before old housewares die, they just might make it out to Westbury. Here are used and new pots, pans, dishes, glassware, toilet seats, and nearly anything you might need for your home, including large and small furniture. This is the largest job-lot center in the tri-state region; King Arthur's buys up stores, estates, and truckloads that were not accepted at their destinations.

If you happen to be on Long Island and want to do some "stocking up" for your kitchen and bathroom, there's another multilevel outlet that salvages defunct houseware stores and sells everything in stock dirt cheap: **San Salvage Store** (70 M. J. Boulevard, Brentwood, 516/231-6888; 2100 Broad Hollow Road, Farmingdale, 516/249-1818; American Express, MC, Visa.)

And be sure to bring a van or truck to King Arthur's or San Salvage, for you may well want to get carried away.

LECHTER'S HOUSWARES & GIFTS
55 East Eighth Street (505-0576);
2503 Broadway (864-5464); 901 Sixth Avenue (268-7303); 1198 Third Avenue (744-1427)
American Express, Visa, MC

You will marvel at the great buys to be found in the dependable houseware store called Lechter's, already a phenomenon in other parts of the country but just beginning to rev up here. From every size picture frame, starting at $.99, to some fifty varieties of clothes hangers, many that cost $1, you can shop here all day.

Purchase heavy-duty garbage bags for $.69; replacement coffee pots for $8.99; gold-plated napkin holders for $2; and an assortment of microwavable containers for just $3.99. I was happy to see a fun assortment of kids' toys and necessities and a whopping twenty-two different beverage pitchers starting at $2.99!

If this isn't enough, look at their unique dish and platter assemblage; the oak spice rack for $25; Combat "roach motels" for $1.99; and a series of colorful potato peelers for $1.55. Lechter's is one of the few all-inclusive houseware stores in the five boroughs that painstakingly prices each and every item. It can save you time! Lechter's happily announces its price breaks; the "original" costs are marked and crossed out and consumer values are printed underneath.

For another place to stock up, go to **Canal Self Service Store** (395 Broadway, 966-3069), where in addition to selling household goods, they will develop your 35mm film for $1.88.

FOUNTAIN PEN HOSPITAL
10 Warren Street
964-0580
American Express, MC, Visa

Everything to satisfy your writing needs in the best-stocked pen store in Manhattan: fountain pens, ballpoint collections, lead pencils, Magic Markers, and a full line of Pilot pens. This highly-touted stationery store (also called F.P.H. Office Products) sells $.99/dozen Paper Mate ballpoints and it also carries such diverse product lines as Stel-co organizer/portfolios for $34.95, SlimLine Day Runners for $14.95, and quality table fans for $39.95.

These are but a few examples from this modern stationery store, a tiny neighborhood outlet that sells discounted office knickknacks and items you might be surprised to find here, including vertical file holders and home-office supplies like wall dividers and copiers. As the name suggests, Fountain Pen Hospital also fixes wounded pens.

Thomas Parker's best writing instruments start at $85 and a $69 Pelican pen makes an excellent gift. Ask about bulk rates on fountain and rollerball pens.

BROADWAY PANHANDLER
520 Broadway
966-3434
American Express, MC, Visa

In a mecca of junk-clothing stores along lower Broadway you will run into a complete kitchen store that offers professional quality cookware and a fine selection of cooking accessories.

Calphalon and Wearever aluminum pots and a host of stainless steel pots are sold at this well-heeled shop for 30 percent off regular prices. You can save 20 percent off the list prices on an excellent stock of imported knives by Wustoff and Sabatier; same goes for the domestic brands that include Lamson & Goodnow and Russell Harrington. They also carry dishes, silverware, and . . . Tupperware!

FREEDA VITAMINS
36 East 41st Street
685-4980
MC, Visa
Closed Saturday and Sunday

Since 1928, this family-run pharmacy has produced vitamins devoid of dyes, sulfates, animal stearates, pesticides, sugar, and artificial flavorings. Save around 40 per-

cent off the other manufacturers' prices on mult
minerals, and nutritional products. The minerals
at this store are too many to name, but some sa...p... ...
calcium, iron, potassium, zinc, amino acids, proteins, sele-
nium, and additive-free germs! In the back, too, is a special section devoted to children's vitamins.

POTTERY BARN
**Locations throughout the five boroughs, upstate New
York, Long Island, New Jersey, and Connecticut
505-6377
American Express, MC, Visa
Some suburban stores closed Sunday**

"The store for today's home" is the well-intentioned
slogan for Pottery Barn. Really, you get decent prices on
the finest array of glassware, summer products (hammocks, fans, tables and chairs), flatware, nesting trays and
party buckets, mats, drawer placemats, tiny rugs, kitchen
jugs, napkin holders, butter dishes, toasters and small appliances, mugs, stools, potholders, mixing bowls, wine de-
canters, and a host of unlikely specialty products that pop
up from time to time. Also, the stores lower their prices
on a particular line each week because their credo is to
have something at discount at all times.

Keep Pottery Barn in mind when you need to buy a
wedding gift for the hard-to-please. (For more ideas, see
chapter 22, "Novelties and Gift Items.") For instance,
look to the Margarita glasses and see a complementing tin
of sea-salt!

In Manhattan there is a plethora of these fancily dec-
orated chain stores. There are so many they need to have
a special store just to sell the discontinued merchandise
from last season, often at tremendous savings. (**Pottery
Barn Warehouse**, 231 10th Avenue, 2nd Floor, 206-8118;
American Express, MC, Visa.)

UMBRELLAS

Now for some fun:

◆ **Essex Umbrella Corporation** (101 Essex Street, 674-3394) offers a 20 percent discount on Knirps and Totes umbrellas.

◆ **Salwen Umbrellas** (45 Orchard Street, 226-1693) has a 30 percent discount on Knirps, London Fog, Oscar de la Renta, Vera, Pierre Cardin, and the American brand Totes. They have rainhats, too, and very good prices.

◆ **Gloria Umbrella Manufacturing Company** (39 Essex Street, 475-7388), is one of the oldest New York umbrella stores on record. In their very small space they still stock every kind of imported and domestic umbrella, though you won't find the $2 ones they sell on the street. Every piece can, if you request, be "custom designed."

◆ **Stanley Novak Company** (115 West 30th Street, 947-8466) offers 20 percent off on Knirps and even more of a discount on standards. Umbrella aficionados tell me that Novak carries the best handles in town!

◆ **Hanae Mori** (27 East 79th Street, 472-2352; American Express, MC, Visa) is not that cheap but still sells folding umbrellas that are so elegant you'll wonder whether the designer Mori makes matching silk shirts (she doesn't). The brollies are $85.

◆ See **Totes Factory Outlet** in chapter 5, "Shop-by-Mail."

THE CLAY POT
**162 Seventh Avenue, Park Slope, Brooklyn, take "2/3"
to Grand Army Plaza
718/788-6564
American Express, MC, Visa**

Bob and Sally Silberg's 1,200 square foot store houses

ceramic, wood, and glass objects from nearly seven hundred artisans from all over this country. They have everything from housewares to perfume bottles (though you can buy the latter for almost nothing at **Jerry's Job Lot,** 9 West 17th Street, 741-1632; closed Saturday and Sunday). I was impressed with Clay Pot's jewelry. How about a hand-dipped candle for $5?

GREATER NEW YORK TRADING COMPANY
81 Canal Street
226-2808
American Express, MC, Visa

One of the more unlikely stores on the block, Greater Trading stands amid a collection of *tschachke* shops and stereo centers. It, too, has small appliances and refrigerators, but also one of the best stocks of china in town! You'll find crystal stemware by Block, Kosta Boda, Val St. Lambert, and Waterford, and an assortment of discontinued patterns, in addition to knickknacks for a homier china cabinet.

CHAPTER 18

Luggage and Carry-Alls

ALTMAN LUGGAGE
135 Orchard Street
254-7275
American Express, MC, Visa
Closed Saturday

Altman is set up like a schlock shop. They don't list prices and are anxious to move their inventory quickly. That means they're always happy to have you haggle them down. For a west-side example of this phenomenon, see **Toyon Leather Shop,** (158 Church Street, 227-1880; American Express, MC, Visa; closed Sunday) which runs regular specials on Samsonite and will bargain with you, too.

As for Altman, you'll be glad you talked to the trained salesmen, because they know their stock and sell quality brands like American Tourister, Samsonite, Ventura, and Hartmann. These are side by side with the Boyt Bags from Iowa Falls, all at savings of up to 50 percent.

Also find newfangled closet bags and a selection of fine pens that rivals **Staples'**. See chapter 17, "Stationery and Household Items." Best to pay cash for a heftier discount.

BER-SEL HANDAGS
79 Orchard Street
966-5517
American Express, MC, Visa
Closed Saturday

Here are cases, gloves, and so many handbags you'll think you're in handbag heaven. Ber-sel features year-round savings of 35 percent and always a special sales rack where prices are cut an additional 20 percent.

A TO Z LUGGAGE
Locations include 425 Fifth Avenue, 703 Third Avenue, 6 East 23rd Street, 26 Broadway, 790 Seventh Avenue, and, in Brooklyn, a spacious outlet at 4627 New Utrecht Avenue
718/435-2880
Closed Saturday and on Broadway closed Sunday
American Express, MC, Visa

A luggage store that doubles as a place to purchase the perfect gift for the hard-to-please: Find fun items such as a director's chair paperclip holder, engravable, for $15; a "nose" to sit your glasses on, for $10; a tiny battery-operated fan, for $12.50; and must-have office supplies such as an "executive basketball hoop" for $35 and a sports bookmark. Oh, and luggage: A to Z sells portfolios (as low as $49.95 for shoulder pouch/compartment models), high-tech attachés in black (starting at $180) or the Samsonite Oyster collection of wheeled units (featured at $97.99). These are not the absolute best prices, but undoubtedly the largest selection of the pioneering concepts in luggage. Special sales, advertised through the mail, go on for weeks.

Buy a travel raincoat in its own pouch for $10, or a hide-a-pocket wallet to nestle comfortably in your belt loop for $13.50. They also specialize in Hartmann office cases and wallets at a discount (hard to find at low prices). Ads state they beat the competition on American Tourister and Andiamo; you have to bring the better price with you.

THE CHOCOLATE SOUP
946 Madison Avenue
861-2210
American Express, MC, Visa

Come here for the "classic Danish" expandable bag, namely the $75 model that has many compartments. The rest of their merchandise is pretty expensive, though their name is about as terrific as California's **The Kitchen Sink,** and the fun stuff inside is worth a trip to Madison Avenue.

ACE LEATHER
2211 Avenue U in Sheepshead Bay, Brooklyn
Take "D/Q" to Avenue U
718/645-3534
American Express, MC, Visa
Closed Sunday

This is the only shop I know that has five full stockrooms at *one location.* In addition, all the stock here is reportedly 35 percent below retail. When there's overstock they break the bank and raise the discount to 50 percent! But better than that is their refreshing attitude: At Ace they beat anyone's price without an argument (see **A to Z** above). They stock all small leather goods, including classic handbags by Aigner, Dooney & Burke, and Liz Claiborne. Of the latter, they beat the prices listed at the factory outlets in New Jersey and upstate New York (see chapters 6 and 10). Large-size luggage brands include Ventura, Wings, Fulton of France, American Tourister, and Lark.

They will send you a catalogue. (Phone and mail orders are especially welcome if you know which model you want.)

CARNEGIE LUGGAGE
1288 Sixth Avenue
586-8210
American Express, MC, Visa
Closed Sunday

This midtown travel supply shop specializes in popular brands of luggage, and gives a good price on Delsey units from Paris that are made of tough aluminum, the material in the sides of airplanes. Oddities found here include briefcases by Samsonite at 20 percent off; a fine grouping of the pricey Zero Halliburton expandable cases; and "pilot cases," also made of aluminum, for $160. Shoulder bags are discounted.

Considering nobody expects places in the Carnegie Hall area to be cheap, this one will surprise you with its selection and prices: for instance, they have garment bags starting at $90, and a shelf lined with cigarette cases starting at $10.

For briefcases, also see **Staples** (chapter 17); "Stationery and Household Items."

THE TRADER
385 Canal Street
925-6610
American Express, MC, Visa

If you're out and about in the city all day, you're likely to want to carry a few personal items with you in a small bag, such as a knapsack or carry-all. The Trader is the place where, for around $8, you are destined to find a bag to match your personality. They carry everything from new and used shoulder packs to a case for a cello or a gun. In addition, Trader prides itself on selling the finest wartime accessories such as holders for grenades and other "stylish" merchandise.

They sell tiny belt pouches, and wallets, too, but not the classy kind of either. For an $8–$18 men's or women's wallet, visit the well-established **Elite Shoe Repair** (105 West 10th Street, 243-0951; 971 First Avenue, 759-9266; closed Sunday).

THE BAG HOUSE
797 Broadway
260-0940
American Express, MC, Visa

Have you ever wanted a bag that could last your whole life? Well, the Eagle Creek duffel bag is here, and it can be found at the Bag House, which carries the full line. It comes in many colors and is guaranteed for life ($50–$70).

The Bag House is not the best-priced store, but all their merchandise is of the finest quality and most innovative. While many luggage shops have a tacky appearance, at Bag House everything is so colorful and fashionable that it's fun just to browse.

Also sold at this deceptively small store are tiny items for travel such as money belts, a holder for sanitary toilet covers, and an amazing collection of Day-Glo backpacks starting at $35. They sell hip pouches in many colors, starting at $12. (A smooth leather pouch is available around town for $15–$18; seek out the simple tanned-leather store **Ananias** (all over Manhattan, 695-2052; American Express, MC, Visa).

Bag House features JanSport bags and backpacks, all containing a new gimmick called a "key-per." Inside each bag is a strap you attach your keys to—a mighty secure addendum. Other items of interest are the Caribou shoulder holders for $15; Club USA pouches for just $2.98; a "journey bag" in a multitude of sizes for around $150; and a cleverly devised Organizer by Jasper for school, with so many pockets inside you could feasibly get lost.

LAST-MINUTE LUGGAGE

Clearances are often held for women's leather bags at the **Village Tannery** (173 Bleecker, 673-5444; 742 Broadway, 979-0013; American Express, MC, Visa) and, for men, at **E. Vincent Luggage Shop** (1420 Sixth Avenue, 752-8251; American Express, MC, Visa), which discounts many brands of luggage, as well as Schlesinger cases, made of discontinued saddle leather, by 40 percent.

AMERICAN TOURISTER FACTORY OUTLET
Suite 61, 3163 Outlet Boulevard, Myrtle Beach, SC 29577
803/236-7787
MC, Visa

Now that you've read a chapter that includes many places to buy American Tourister—and perused two chapters (6, "New Jersey" and 10, "Upstate World") that sang the praises of various American Tourister factory outlets—it's time to discover a way to get it even cheaper: through the mail. Elysa Lazar, publisher of a monthly guide on shopping through the mail (see coupon in the back) says the American Tourister mail-order center can grant you 40–70 percent off on their entire range of quality luggage. If you know what you want, and have the color and 4-digit series number, give the factory outlet a call and compare their prices to the stores'. If you are planning to purchase Tourister this season, it could be a golden opportunity. According to the Carolina-based company, you can expect to see the luggage on your door-step in five days!

For more luggage, see chapter 5, "Shop-by-Mail."

CHAPTER 19

Furniture

Furniture merchants are listed throughout this book, but this chapter presents certain key places that must be seen for *extra special* values.

Some of these are out-of-the-ordinary sales, others are just good buys. But most important, remember not to buy furniture on a whim, as it's likely to be something that will be with you for a long time. Furniture can have as high as a 600 percent markup, another reason to look hard and long at each piece you consider. As mentioned in chapter 8, "Brooklyn the Eclectic," and chapter 23, "Those Answered Questions," it might be a good idea to buy something in not-quite-stellar shape, and fix it yourself (or find someone to do the work). You may save a veritable bundle.

FOREMOST FURNITURE
8 West 30th Street
889-6347

Foremost is a savings center advertising so-called "double sales"—in which they double their normal discount—on a regular basis. I advise furniture lovers to get on their mailing list immediately. Every month or so they send out a nondescript postcard with necessary details. You just have to show up. Their regular prices, meanwhile, constitute a 70 percent discount on regular stock like living room sets, leather couches, upholstered sofas and convertibles, and other gallery pieces, including armoires listing at $5,000, which you will find at regular "sale" prices of just over $2000.

Foremost has a Clearance Center at 653 11th Avenue, 3rd floor (889-6347), where you can get leftovers from perhaps a month ago. Brands include Thomasville, Bernhardt, Henredon, and Stanley, and the sales they hold include many items sold below cost.

Need more reasons to shop at Foremost? When they can get them they have fossil-stone dining tables, normally sold for $1,650, cut to $785. An eleven-piece dining room set retailing at $7,800 will go for $3,985 during the sale. Queen sofa beds by Sealy Posturepedic Beekman, normally $950, will come down during a regular sale to $485. Floor samples are sold as is, and are negotiable. See coupon in the back.

IKEA
1000 Center Drive, Elizabeth, New Jersey
201/289-4488 (New Jersey Transit bus from New York: 564-8484)
American Express, MC, Visa

One of the hippest ways to shop is naturally one of the newest. Ikea is a giant shopping mall just for furniture—and boy is it cheap! All furniture is designed in Sweden and it covers every room in the house (even those you may not have thought of).

They have no overhead because they have no salespeople. Their apt slogan is, "We don't want to pay for these guys, so you don't have to pay for these guys!" And the overhead is just the beginning: this Swedish-based outlet has a design catalogue whose prices shock many furniture buyers. (Their other slogan is, "It's a big country, somebody has to furnish it!")

The store, right off the Jersey Turnpike, opened in May as this book was going to press. Its grand opening specials were exemplary of the way they do business—loss leaders mixed in with specialty items that may not be that inexpensive, but you can't find them anywhere else: "Amulett 18-piece tumbler set of cooler, beverage and rock glasses, six of each, for $5." "An *impossible price* of $56 for a Ted-Alex underframe and tabletop." If it's a modern piece you're looking for, you can most likely find it here, have a Swedish snack in the restaurant, browse for hours—there's no one to ask, "May I help you?"—pick up your purchases at the self-serve warehouse, and live happily ever after with your furniture.

JENSEN-LEWIS CO.
—1496 Third Avenue, 439-6440
—89 Seventh Avenue, 929-4880
American Express, MC, Visa, checks

Once located on Ninth Avenue, these more upscale Jensen-Lewises offer easy living "knock-down" furniture at just fair prices. But since you can't find a canvas director's chair in 28 colors *anywhere else,* you might as well come here! Also come for other styles of easy-to-afford canvas chairs, duffle bags, folding screens, hammocks, dop kits, and canvas at $7 per yard to make your own furniture with. Recently they added a popular children's director's chair for just $30.

URBAN ARCHEOLOGY
137 Spring Street
431-6969
American Express, MC, Visa

The *tschachkes* sold here are called "urban architectural artifacts," and include old cash registers, wooden doors, wooden toilet seats, gargoyles, columns, fireplace grates, and ancient soda fountains. Unlike other novelty furniture stores, Urban does not believe in either dropping the prices or removing items after they've sat in the store a while. So a set of Tiffany stained-glass windows from a church in upstate New York stayed around for years.

The prices for this type of artifact are noticeably lower than at other downtown stores where such furniture is popular. You can haggle, too.

CONRAN'S
160 East 54th Street
371-2225
American Express, MC, Visa

The Conran stores started in London, Paris, and Brussels years ago under the name of Habitat. They moved here and soon found that they could not compete—not with their originally expensive price range. So they cut down the merchandise, all well-designed and brightly colored, so that today you can find an extra touch, at a good price, at the modern Conran's. This is the store to go to for good-looking accessories. There are other chain stores that sell basically the same *type* of furniture—**Door Store** is a popular chain (for locations throughout the five boroughs call 679-9700). The problem with Door Store is that they sell cheap stuff that falls apart before its time.

Designs at Conran's are streamlined, and stock changes day to day. Table tops with small frame and legs of pine cost around $400, and sofas, occasional tables, chairs, stools, and shelf units are beautiful, bountiful, and even bargains! Conran's continually adds stock; in the course of one year they added lines of espresso cups, aprons, pasta machines, jams, mustards, and teas.

Other Manhattan locations (not as well stocked as the uptown branch) are 2248 Broadway, 873-9250, and 2 Astor Place, 505-1515.

NAGA ANTIQUES
167 East 61st Street
593-2788
Checks accepted
Closed Sunday

This stop has an expensive collection of Orientalia such as screens, textiles, ceramics, and lacquerware. However, they have some smaller items, and you may well happen upon a good deal at this ordinarily high-priced shop. It's a fun stop for every furniture aficionado, regardless of the budget. Design buffs know that upper east side decorators buy just the right touches for their clients' apartments here. And department store windows fill up with items from Naga.

CURTIS FURNITURE COMPANY
40 East 19th Street
673-5353
American Express, MC, Visa
Closed Sunday

Book stacks are on sale constantly at Curtis Company.

What are book stacks? They're cases that stack, in all heights, shapes, and textures. Models that are made to order are more expensive.

BON MARCHE
Warehouse: 55 West 13th Street, 620-5588
Branch: 1060 Third Avenue, 620-5592
MC, Visa
Closed Sunday

This famous store, which has branches in the Midwest, features designer-stock sofas, beds, dining room sets, and book shelves. The good news is that they are always moving merchandise, so prices drop weekly. The bad news is they charge a lot for delivery—so rent a U-Haul or bring friends.

CARPETING

ABC Carpet is the best place to buy carpet in New York City, because it's a civilized place to shop and—most crucially—the prices are unbeatable. At 881 and 888 Broadway (473-3000, major credit cards accepted) they sell hundreds of rolls of broadloom carpeting on nine floors, ranging from low-end synthetics to $100-per-square-yard wools (including installation). Discontinued lines are sold at about 20 percent below list price. At the 888 Broadway branch, find the rug/remnant store, where the main floor is primarily machine-made rugs, with discounts as high as 50 percent off retail prices. Downstairs find handmade Orientals, old and new, at prices ranging from indecently expensive (even discounted) to those at 40 percent less than you could find them elsewhere. ABC is in the process of opening a separate space for Oriental pieces, so hopefully prices and stock will come into line with other merchandise. Also downstairs is an amazing array of remnants, all unpriced: if you know how much a remnant should cost—say, $50 for a 5' by 5'—then you can bargain them down to an even smaller figure. Go to ABC armed with that knowledge.

Additional bargains can be found at various carpet showrooms around town:

- **Redi-Cut Carpets** (22nd Street and Second Avenue, 533-3610, major credit cards accepted) has handmade area rugs, remnants, wall-to-walls, and commercial carpeting at 20 percent lower than retail marts (free padding, too).

- **Carpet Fashions** (111 Fourth Avenue, 673-3801, MC, Visa) has over 6,000 styles of broadloom at about 10 percent lower than what you'll find elsewhere. Hand-knotted rugs are a specialty.

- **Central Carpeting** (426 Columbus, 787-8813, MC, Visa) is *the* place for new rugs from Persia, Turkey, China, India, and Pakistan, allegedly priced "60 percent below appraised value."

- **Rug Tower** (399 Lafayette Street, 677-2525, major credit cards accepted) is an Oriental rug lover's best shopping value. Carpets from Tibet start as low as $2,500, and you'll be noticing a very good discount on Kilims from Turkey and other exotics, too. The cheaper pieces are throw pillows made from old rugs: great gifts and priced reasonably, from $29 to $250.

- For regular auctions of carpet stock, try **The Rug Warehouse** (2222 Broadway, 787-6665, major credit cards accepted), where handmade Orientals and contemporary designs from Europe are regularly acquired for up to 50 percent discount at public biddings. Antique rugs that normally start at $5,000 range at around $3,000 here.

- Carpet cleaning is discounted at the department stores, who do poorly on carpet prices and must offer at least a low-cost cleaning service. Try **Abraham & Straus** (718/854-1717); **Bloomingdale's** (718/389-3500); and **Macy's** (736-5151).

LIGHTING

The best lighting showrooms are located on the Bowery (or lower Third Avenue starting below Houston Street):

- ♦ **Lighting Showroom** (137 Bowery, 431-3880, major credit cards accepted) features Quolzel, Majestic, Illuminating Experiences, Austin Productions, and Paul Hanson, including art lighting designs such as Wedgwood chandeliers and ginger jar lamps, at 50 percent off the list price.

- ♦ **N.Y. Gas Lighting Company** (146 Bowery, 226-2840, MC, Visa) has a fantastic grouping of lamps by Stiffel, Frederick Cooper, and Remington, along with Venetian glass and Capodimonte chandeliers, at 35 to 50 percent off list price. This is the oldest lighting store on the Bowery and the quality is matched by price. Hunter ceiling fans can be had for $225.

- ♦ **Lisa Lighting** (145 Bowery, 966-5825, major credit cards accepted) is a full service outlet with discounts of 30 to 50 percent off list price. Interestingly, the cost of the Tiffany lamps is determined by the number of glass pieces used. Twenty-inch fruit and flower shades are $159.95, and they sell Austrian crystal chandeliers at 40 percent off their expensive list prices. Nutone track lighting sells here for 50 percent off list price.

- ♦ **DAC Lighting Manufacturing** (162-164 and 156 Bowery, 966-7062, major credit cards accepted) sells fixtures at 30 to 50 percent off regular retail; they claim their markup is 40 percent instead of the usual 100 percent. If so, you can find hurricane lamps, crystal chandeliers, and porcelain or brass table lamps of your own design, for something around $250 each. They have expanded so much in the past few years that you can now go to their several show-rooms and still find yourself looking at different items, all at good prices.

In Brooklyn, try **Pintchik Paints** (478 Bergen Street, 718/783-3333, "2/3" to Bergen Street, MC, Visa), a reputable chain store that is more like a fix-it department store. This branch is specifically good for stocking up on fixtures such as track, warehouse shades, paper shades, rice shades, and bamboo hanging fixtures. These items are all selling at around 50 percent off. And unlike other Pintchiks, here you can also find unusual pharmacy lamps and the Puritan, Supreme, and Popular Mobilite, at a third off the Manhattan department store prices.

FUTONS

The best price I have found on quality futon mattresses is the Arise Furniture warehouse in Queens. Because all futons are basically the same, you will want to go to the warehouse showroom of any reputable store. Arise is a chain store with locations throughout the boroughs; and its warehouse showroom is called **Futon Flow**. It is located at 58-25 Laurel Hill Boulevard in Woodside, Queens (718/335-5300, major credit cards accepted, closed Sunday). Flow also has a location in Kew Gardens (81-65 Lefferts Boulevard, 718/846-8500, major credit cards accepted, open seven days). Futons start at $49, frames at $99! Whenever they have a sale, delivery is free.

WICKER

♦ **Be Seated Inc.** (66 Greenwich Avenue, 924-8444, no

credit cards, checks accepted, closed Sunday) sells moderately priced chairs. They have split-willowed "bentwood" contour lounge chairs for under $100.

♦ **Dan Klemuk's Gazebo** (14 East 57th Street, 832-7077, major credit cards accepted, closed Sunday) features elegant and expensive wicker but does inexpensive custom painting and upholstering for your old pieces. Wicker lamps are priced at $175.

♦ **Deutsch Inc.** (196 Lexington Avenue, 683-8746, major credit cards accepted, closed Sunday) is a wholesaler who sells to private customers. Don't go by the high prices in their catalogue; they will bargain with you.

♦ **The Wickery** (342 Third Avenue, 889-3669, closed Sunday, major credit cards accepted) features bucket seat chairs from Poland for about $60, magazine racks from $10, and peel tables for about $20.

LEATHER

New York Furniture Center (41 East 31st Street, 679-8866, MC, Visa only as deposits, checks accepted) features yearly clearance sales on "samples": contemporary bedroom sets, silk-covered sofas, oak dining rooms, and wall systems. The big pieces are reduced by a few thousand dollars when sales are held. Call for details.

Leather furniture sales occur every other month at the **Design Furniture International Showroom** (20th Street and Broadway, 673-8900, MC, Visa). (To find out about private leather sales, get on their mailing list.) "To appreciate fine leather you must feel it" is their motto. And to see a sectional discounted 35 percent to $900, you must visit Design Furniture, which has recently expanded. They offer free remodeling design consultation.

EARLY TWENTIES SCAVENGING

If you want to go out and see the latest furniture designs before you decide on an actual make and model, check out the champions of the furniture district along West 20th and 21st Streets between Sixth and Park Avenues. Here you can see over fifteen expensive furniture retailers, and you will have a better idea of recent makes and models. Then price them at the phone sales centers named above.

CHAPTER 20

Home Appliances

This Chapter is about necessities for the home and office.

You are not ready to shop for these products until you have an exact make and model number of the appliance you need (camera, turntable, sewing machine, computer, etc.). In order to get the best price possible, it is imperative that you shop around. The places in this chapter are ready to give you the lowest price they can, but they ask first that you not waste their time. If shoppers know what they want, they help keep overhead, and prices, low.

FOTO ELECTRIC SUPPLY COMPANY
31 Essex Street
673-5222
MC, Visa

This small Lower East Side shop is not the easiest

place to shop in. Like many of the others in this chapter, they want you to have the exact model number—or at least a precise idea of what you want—before you come in. They will give you "attitude" if you walk in ignorant.

Two brothers named Sol run the store, hawking cheap Polaroids and almost all makes of 35mm cameras, telephones, and assorted accessories, electronic oddities, perfumes, and anything to make a modern gadget lover happy. Their prices are below normal discount even for the Lower East Side, where shops still offer their merchandise for less than wholesale.

Foto Electric forgoes image for stock—merchandise is piled up everywhere. When I asked whether it bothered people, one employee said, "Not the people who shop here."

UNCLE STEVE
343 Canal Street
226-4010
American Express, MC, Visa

This might be thought just another Crazy Eddie, the defunct, unglamorous place whose advertisements announced "We will not be undersold." But truthfully, while that chain was in existence, his lesser known Uncle—no relation—couldn't be beat. Steve's prices are not insanely low, but unlike "Eddie," they're listed right on the labels. The sales clerks don't go out of their way to be popular—uncannily, their ad states, "I Love You"—but their prices are worth a little unpleasantness.

Answering machines, portable computers—even Sharp Wizard and the like—computer printers, stereos, and all sorts of electronic gadgetry are sold here at discount prices (usually a notch above wholesale). After you get a straight answer out of the clerk about price, you will actually feel like you have an uncle in the business. At press time they were selling the new Casio Boss—a typewriter version of the Sharp Wizard—for $169, half what it sells for elsewhere.

There's another location for Uncle Steve (216 West 72nd Street, 874-3317; American Express, MC, Visa) but their prices are higher.

SAVE-A-THON
Locations in Manhattan (369-4453): 1887 Third Avenue; 256 West 125th Street
Locations in Brooklyn (718/852-5757): 411 Bridge Street; 393 Bridge Street; 824 Flatbush Avenue; and 24 Graham Avenue
American Express, MC, Visa

There is no better place for zig-zag, serger, and standard model sewing machines, particularly since the tried-and-true Singer Company is out of business. (Some Singer stores remain; they are franchised, though, so their prices aren't very good.) In addition to the above, Save-a-Thon has other locations throughout the Bronx and Brooklyn. For mail orders, phone the Brooklyn number; add $10 for UPS shipping. Up to 75 percent off manufacturer's list price can be found at Save-a-Thon on brands including Simplicity, Nelco, Brother, and, yes, Singer machines.

SIXTH AVENUE ELECTRONICS CITY
1060 Sixth Avenue
575-1849
Also 331 Route 4 North, Paramus, New Jersey (201/489-0666)
American Express, MC, Visa
Closed Sunday

The Crazy Eddie spokesman, Jerry Carroll, has softened his act in order to hawk products for the quiet and carpeted Sixth Avenue, which does little advertising and no grandstanding about their truly good prices and quality merchandise.

It is nice to stop in here merely to see how pleasant salespeople can be. True, they do not list any prices—you have to discuss them with the sales help—but here, unlike Carroll's former employer, they will not badger you into buying something you don't need. (I have seen the sales people drift over to something they "prefer." It was unclear whether it was because of higher price or quality.)

All name brands are here, and an exceptional selection of Sony products. Downstairs, in their soundproof mini-showroom, you will notice a fireplace. It's very homey—that's the idea. Emerson and Federated air conditioners are on sale all year round. They also hold special sales regularly on individual stereo components, such as speakers, receivers, turntables, and old-model CD players. See below for a warning about extended warranties.

DEMBITZER BROTHERS
5 Essex Street
254-1310
American Express, MC, Visa
Closed Saturday

I love how these people advertise their electronics market: "Shop at one of the oldest discount houses on the Lower East Side—we speak eight languages." Not meaning to burst their bubble, but nearly every store that exists on the Lower East Side has been there since the early part of the century, and they all speak many languages (e.g., Yiddish, Polish, Hebrew, Spanish, and Portuguese). The difference is Dembitzer has all the other name-brand electrical appliances and the new brands, too.

Still, their flier is the oldest one I know of. It still says they sell air conditioners, refrigerators, tape recorders, calculators, and "Epilady" razors. They give a free imported can opener with every $100 purchase.

Toshiba, Braun, Eureka, Zenith, Sharp, Panasonic, and Farberware are the top of the line at Dembitzers—and the lines of people at the register are just as long. The Dembitzers are proud of their overcrowded store.

See coupon in the back.

THE SHARPER IMAGE
89 South Street Seaport at Pier 17, 693-0477
4 West 57th Street, 265-2550
American Express, MC, Visa

Some shoppers may ask why Sharper Image, an exquisite gadget shop, would be included in a book on bargains. These shops sell pricey robots, video phones, tiny stereos, and adult electronics. Well, they also conduct a floor-model auction every Tuesday at 1 p.m.—and sometimes again on Friday—when a senior salesperson holds up what he or she feels is wasting shelf space.

This sales method is rather subjective, so it might mean the item has languished for a day, a month, or a year. You could get a Sharp Wizard, a mini-stereo, a collapsable pool table, or an automatic blackjack. The bidding starts at half off the regular price.

NEWMARK & LEWIS
Locations throughout the five boroughs:
Call 529-1740
American Express, MC, Visa

Unlike most stereo stores that sell merchandise from their own stock, Newmark & Lewis has the unusual but profitable habit of purchasing stereo stores and selling the other store's stock. They bring the merchandise from various chains to Newmark & Lewis and cut prices on it drastically—this is called "warehousing."

This successful stereo outlet recently bought the entire chain of Brick Church Appliance, and before that, the big suburban collection of Lafayette Electronics. At press time amazing deals were being offered on Sanyo, Awai, and Panasonic stereo units. These compact CD/dual cassette/equalizer/receiver/phonograph sets were going for from $159 to $999. Delivery was $30.

All floor samples are sold, too. These are covered by the warranty normally given to brand-new merchandise.

Finally, the reason Newmark & Lewis stands alone among the competition is that every month a manager gets itchy and throws a one-day sale where nearly everything in the store is slashed by about 50 percent. Recently, the top Citizen computer printers were being sold for $349 "as is." You can be apprised of these one-day events by calling Newmark & Lewis near the end of the month.

OLDEN CAMERA, LENS, VIDEO & COMPUTER STORES
1265 Broadway
725-1234
American Express, MC, Visa

Throughout the West 30s you will find a series of good camera shops. I always say go to Olden because they have the best reputation for honest service, good prices, and instant "deals" if you know how to haggle. On a recent visit I talked them down on a Minolta Maxxum 7000i, usually selling for upwards of $450, to $317 because the salesperson and I talked for an hour. They have all lenses and all makes. And they sell many second-hand and floor models. If you're in the market for camera equipment for a day or a week, they have the best prices on camera rentals (second floor). This is a good option to consider for a party or an adventure on a tropical island.

The best second-hand dealer is **Adorama** (42 West 18th Street, 741-0052; American Express, MC, Visa; closed Sunday), a Minolta and Nikon specialist which thinks of itself as a camera exchange. Just like Olden,

Adorama believes in you telling *them* what you think the model is worth. They like to make bargains. If you're a first time buyer, Adorama is a good place to cut your teeth.

KINGSWAY VIDEO
1690 East 15th Street, Brooklyn
718/998-4700

Kingsway is a fine place to buy video equipment because it was one of the first to offer it some nine years ago. (Today we can nod to a store that was the first to offer D.A.T.—digital tape players: **DAT'S Incredible** [formerly **The DAT Room**], 175 West Fourth Street, 929-7828; MC, Visa.) I think the prices on all Sony brands, including the older Betamaxes, are among the best here. There are VCRs, video cameras, and portapacks, with names like JVC, Panasonic, Emerson, and Sharp. They sell playback VCRs.

Recommended for playback-only fans is **Joy-Lud Electronics** (292 Fifth Avenue, 807-8484), New York's only store dedicated to a Soviet clientele. Here you'll locate beeperless answering machines and hi-fi equipment! The background music is fun.

TRADER HORN
3 East 14th Street
255-8222
other branches throughout the five boroughs
American Express, MC, Visa

I appreciate Trader Horn because they teach us a good lesson about chain stores. They are all over the five boroughs, New Jersey, Long Island, Connecticut, and upstate—but this branch on 14th Street has special prices and loss-leader items such as 19-inch T.V.s for $105. All Trader Horns offer a guarantee: If you find the air conditioner, appliance, Walkman, dishwasher, VCR, or anything you may have purchased there for less somewhere else up to one month after you make the purchase, they will refund the difference.

Prices are low, and clerks are well informed. But beware: the men and women who work at Trader Horn are trained to steer you toward the unnecessary buyer protection plan (see "Three Good Hints," below).

BERNIE'S DISCOUNT CENTER
821 Sixth Avenue
564-8582
American Express, MC, Visa
Closed Sunday

Available at a huge discount at Bernie's are air conditioners, portable stereos, small box fans, self-cleaning ovens, portable compact dryers, and every Hoover and Eureka vacuum cleaner. Here's a store that advertises in all the local papers and through discount fliers—and comes through with great prices. You do well here because Bernie's buys in bulk and reduces prices to keep customers coming back.

Bernie's thinks E.S.P. stands for "extra suction power," but incidentally, the best price on Eureka upright models was found at **Desco Appliance** (131 West 14th Street, 989-1800; American Express, MC, Visa; closed Sunday) which holds regular closeouts on all vacuums. They also repair old models.

PENINSULA BUYING SERVICE
P.O. Box 22
Rockaway Park Station, Rockaway Park, NY 11694
718/945-4100

Unlike many call-in services, Peninsula is run with a conscience. For seventeen years, Steve Cohen, who is handicapped, sold inexpensive home appliances to handicapped consumers. A few years ago he branched out to assist architects and contractors, and as this book went to print he was opening his service to the public. You can call him with the make and model number of your T.V., VCR, oven, air conditioner, stereo unit, exercise equipment, or anything else dreamt up for the home. He will find the best price and will offer a better-priced model ("only once," he cautions).

His prices are about 5 percent above wholesale and he also offers an unusual ten-day at home warranty whereby he will take the piece back and replace it without question.

HOME SALES DIAL-A-DISCOUNT
513-1513; 718/241-3272
Certified checks, bank checks, money orders accepted
Closed Saturday and Sunday

This is one of the finest places to call for air conditioners, major appliances, and even minor ones. Included in the barrel of good prices are washers, dryers, T.V.s, refrigerators, microwaves, stoves, and dishwashers. They guarantee to beat any price you can find, within reason. Get your model number and make and give this place, in operation since 1972, a call.

See chapter 19, "Furniture."

FAXES AND MORE

♦ Fax I: **Bi-Rite Photo and Electronics** (15 East 30th Street, 685-2130; MC, Visa; closed early Friday and all day Saturday) sells phones, answering machines, facsimile machines, and computer printers. You will always do well at Bi-Rite. This establishment is run by Hasidic Jews who believe that everyone deserves a fair price. They do not want to be your friend, they want to know what you are looking for and make you a price offer. You'll find every make and model here, and a good number of top-of-the-line cameras (including many of the newest models).

Bi-Rite was the first to offer major discounts on facsimile machines and have not rested on their laurels—prices of faxes keep dropping. This is the place to shop after you're decided on the exact model you want; they will even ensure that you have brought the right number.

Bi-Rite doesn't play around with prices and will not try to steer you to higher-priced items. They have the best selection of telephone answering machines and the best prices to boot.

♦ Fax II: Super fax prices can be found at a store called **E. 33rd Typewriter and Electronics** (42 East 33rd Street, 686-0930; 478 Sixth Avenue, 463-9494; MC, Visa; prices lower if paid in cash). E. 33rd believes in fax machines by companies such as Murata, Canon, and Epson. Their prices are "the lowest we can afford." They offer them in hopes you'll stay loyal and purchase from their stock of receivers, camcorders, air conditioners, etc.

♦ Fax III: **Faxland** (62 West 22nd Street, 633-0035; American Express, MC, Visa) has specials on Sharp. They buy certain low-priced models in bulk and slash the price. A well-stocked fax-only showroom, Faxland is a place to test out fax machines and learn about them. They have good prices on leased faxes.

PLACES TO PRICE MERCHANDISE

♦ **The Wiz** must think people don't know the difference between list price and their price: In ads they say an item is "now $39.95 when it lists for $69.95." But list prices for stereo and electronic equipment are expected to be around 40 percent higher than the actual pricetags.

The Wiz sells Walkmans at loss-leader prices—often as low as $15. Be careful of the overzealous salespeople. All makes and models are stocked, and showrooms are in each store. (Locations: 289-8800, American Express, MC, Visa).

♦ Go to **J & R Music World** to price stereos, individual speakers and components, and computers. The main store at 23 Park Row, across from City Hall, is perfect for "just looking." Also see the computer store next door at 16 Park Row (732-8600; American Express, MC, Visa; closed Sunday). For mail order information, see chapter 5, "Shop-by-Mail."

THREE GOOD HINTS

♦ Although we speak of great closeout specials in this chapter, be careful of a place famous for "every item sold below cost for 12 hours." Called **Tops Appliance City,** with several locations in New Jersey, they promise you amazing deals on air conditioners and refrigerators. Somehow, each time I've arrived, the items had just sold out—some five minutes after the 12 hours began.

♦ Be careful about extra protection plans, which offer you one to three years' "service" for extra money. This is how electronics stores make big money. In most cases you are better off putting the $79 in the bank and using the money and the interest to pay for any repairs you might incur. If your machine breaks *five* years later, by then your extra warranty has run out. For more information, write to Consumer Information Center, Service Contracts, Dept. 82, Pueblo, CO 81009.

♦ Computers and typewriters are best bought after you know the exact make and model number. Look at your friends' models or see the ones at **47th Street Photo** (67 West 47th Street; 115 West 45th Street; 116 Nassau Street; 1976 Hempstead Turnpike, Long Island; information, 260-4415; American Express, MC, Visa; some stores closed Saturday). After you have priced the merchandise, purchase it from computer wholesalers, many of whom will make good deals if you know what you want. They can be found in the yellow pages under "Computer Sales." Or skip the process and buy a second-hand unit from well-known **National Computer Exchange** (118 East 25th Street, 614-0700; MC, Visa; closed Saturday and Sunday), a network of computer experts.

CHAPTER 21

Services and Unusual Bargains

This is a chapter about services (and some unusual extras) you are likely to need while living or shopping in New York. Try these places out, and if you need more information about any of them call up and ask for a catalogue, brochure, or flier.

And while we're on the subject of calling, I don't want to pass up the chance to save you a little money: Calling from a payphone, 25¢, is cheaper if you use MCI and speak for less than two minutes. It's the only credit card at press time that does not add a surcharge for minimal local use. The savings—13¢—may seem trivial, but if you are running around New York trying to hunt down bargains, it can certainly add up.

PRICE CLUB
3000 Middle Country Road, Nesconset, Long Island
(516/366-1500)
1101 Sunrise Highway, Copague, Long Island
Also in Northhaven, Connecticut (203/234-8627) and
Edison, New Jersey (201/287-2667)
Closed Sunday

With a business license or company affiliation (credit

union or private club membership), you can become a member of this unique buying service: After paying $25 for a membership, come in and enjoy the bargains. Some of them are unbeatable, because Price Club makes good deals with manufacturers and distributors. You will find stereos, calculators, paper goods, hardware, furnishings, shoes and clothing, gardening and houseware supplies, and much more. And you can even bring a guest.

HAROLD REUTER FOREIGN EXCHANGE COMPANY
200 Park Avenue
661-0826
American Express, MC, Visa
Closed Sunday

Unlike most European cities, in New York it is not easy to find private places that change money. So you go to banks. You can, however, get the best rates of exchange at the Harold Reuter establishment. They change their rates during the day instead of reestablishing them each morning.

THE WHOLESALE ART GROUP OF MORSE HARRIS
334 East 59th Street
980-4457
American Express, MC, Visa
Closed Sunday

Here's an unusual way to obtain a collection of fine art: a warehouse of artwork! There's a wide selection *and* good prices, and art is being sold by a reputable source. Wholesale prices, sanctioned by the artists or their estates, from names such as Delacroix, Yamagatta, Haring, Stella, and more. Get the picture in mind and then come up and see them sometime.

CHANG'S GALLERY
197 Seventh Avenue
627-0809
Checks accepted

Mr. Chang teaches Tai-Chi-Chuan and frames your picture. He is one of the few framers who cuts the price down to the bare minimum. His prices are negotiable, and his frame selection is fairly good. (Be sure not to leave your print there too long; it's one large dusty room.) Keep in mind that a regular custom framing job that might cost you $80 at a fancy place would be around $30–$35 at Chang's.

For people who want to frame-it-yourself, see the coupon in the back for the relatively inexpensive **Chelsea Frames** (194 Eighth Avenue, 807-8957; MC, Visa). They assist you in framing your valuables and whimsical prints and documents. By loaning you the tools you are spared the cost of labor.

GRIECOS CAR RENTAL
3110 Queens Boulevard, Long Island City
Take "7" to 33rd Street
718/361-3050
American Express, MC, Visa

Formally Value, Griecos has some of the rudest help in the five boroughs, but for $29 a day you can put up with it. Make your reservations at least *two weeks* ahead of time, and do not expect a car on the weekend unless you are taking it for the whole weekend. They are strict about this policy.

Also in Long Island City, **Grieco's Van Rental** (31-10 Queens Boulevard, 718/361-3050; American Express, MC, Visa) rents mini-cargo vans for $19.95 per day, plus $.35/mile.

DISCOUNT COURIERS

♦ One company has proven itself cheap, but it's not

really on the ball: **Discount Couriers** (769-9701)
bring your package within the first zone (First t
86th Streets in Manhattan) for $4.95. The catch is, you
will be billed a minimum charge of $35 a month *or*
must place a $100 deposit with their organization.

♦ An inexpensive courier I can recommend, not as
"dirt cheap" as Discount Courier, is **Unique Courier**
(800/287-8177). They say they charge $3.99 for any
run, but there are hidden surcharges on the bill such
as "bicyclist had to wait at light: 45¢." They require
advance payment or C.O.D. Unique's prices are negotiable if you become a good customer.

DISCOUNT PARKING

♦ The best deal I could find is **GGMC Parking** (503-
519 10th Avenue, 564-1139) which will charge
$87.50 for one month if you negotiate with them.

♦ If you can handle the neighborhood, try **Parking Garage, Inc.** (26 Little West 12th Street, one block below 13th Street, 233-1220) which will charge
between $100 and $125 for a month, and $50 week-
ly. (Weekly rates are hard to find.)

♦ **GMC Garage Management** (50th Street and Broadway, and 57th Street and Eleventh Avenue, 888-
7400) charges between $125 and $169 and is a dependable lot. All of the above are indoor parking
garages and all charge an additional (aboveboard)
18.25 percent New York State tax.

THE COMPLETE COLLEGIATE, INC.
490 Route 46 East, Fairfield, New Jersey
Mail orders by catalogue: 201/882-9339
American Express, MC, Visa, checks

Every time I read about this place I have to laugh:

*ompany specifically for the college-
ty not? Find here special bargains on
:ncil sharpeners, all-inclusive tool kits,
hotpots with tea bags and hot choco-
te. Directions: Take the Lincoln Tunnel
st on Route 46, and make a U-turn to
rter mile and see the annex in back of
the Marvel building. Get on their mailing list for notice
of their private sales.

NORMAN J. SEAMAN'S CONCERT CLUB
130 St. Edwards Street, #7-A, Brooklyn
718/855-9293
Checks accepted

This bargain-basement concert-theater club is perfect
for those who like to attend small concerts. A grass-roots
institution founded in the '50s, Seaman's offers free tickets to some fifty music and theater performances a month,
and often adds in film screenings and closed lectures. Annual dues are $39.95. See coupon in the back.

MYSTIC COLOR LAB
P.O. Box 144, Mystic, CT 06355
800/367-6061

I am amazed that more people don't stop using the
costly one-hour photo places—and now the new, more
expensive thirty-minute photo places—in favor of Mystic
Color. In about two days (they pay postage) you have
sharp photos which are going to make you feel doubly
good: Your pictures are beautiful, one. And two, you've
gotten, say, a roll of twenty-four exposures developed for
just $5.95. Figure that regular Kodak developing is, at
best, $10.59! Write or call for free security mailers.

UNUSUAL FEDERAL SALES

Federal surplus goods are sold at government auctions. Here's how it works: These goods were used for two to ten years and are about to be replaced by the government. Before the goods are made available to the public, however, the General Services Agency must first offer them to other agencies; if they're rejected you can bid for them. Expect to find vehicles, furniture, and heavy equipment used by the government for, well governing. . . .

◆ **General Services Auctions** (26 Federal Plaza, 264-2034).

◆ **Department of Defense Auctions** (26 Federal Plaza, 264-3300).

◆ **United States Customs Auctions** (Pier A, Port Authority; or even better, 11 Westside Avenue, Jersey City, New Jersey, 405/357-9194).

PHONE SERVICES

Free things are among the best on earth. So dial away these free phone services:

◆ **Brooklyn Botanic Garden** has a helpful plant information line (718/622-4440).

◆ The **Movie Line** (777-FILM) gives tips on current hit films.

◆ A reputable **Dance & Music Hotline** (382-2323) can help eradicate feelings of boredom.

◆ The **Sleep Hotline** (439-2992) will get you snoozing.

◆ Taped **Headlines** (718/921-6600; international news is extension 6501, state and local news is 6502, business and local political races are at extension 6504) keep you informed at the push of a button.

- **Sky Reporter** at Hayden Planetarium (769-5917) is beautiful for starry, starry nights.

- **Tel Consumer** (732-8400) will give advice on consumer issues.

- **Tel-Med** (732-8400) has taped medical advice around the clock.

- **Dial-a-Dinner** (838-6644) will tell you about restaurants throughout Manhattan.

- And my favorite, **New York's Visitors Bureau** (397-8222), will help stimulate your cultural appetite.

NOW VOYAGER FREELANCE COURIERS
74 Varick Street
431-1616
MC, Visa
Closed Sunday; limited office hours

Going to Paris tonight? Berlin tomorrow? Try hopping on a courier flight. The basics are as follows: The courier service wants luggage space on commercial flights. You offer yours to the service and they'll cut your ticket sometimes by half—sometimes more. You fly coach and travel round trip for a specified time. On international flights, you are the first one let off the plane. All of this is on the level, but you have to be willing to travel with hand luggage only.

Now Voyager has special "urgent courier needs," so if you call their hotline (431-1666) after the office closes, you will hear a recording about what flights are leaving shortly (often the next day). For instance, "We need someone to go to Hong Kong—cost $100 roundtrip." Instant vacation! Yearly registration fee is required. See coupon in the back.

Halbart Air Service is the newest courier service, with $289–$350 round trip fares to most European cities.

Couriers should order four-to-six weeks ahead—no registration fee (718/656-8279, extensions 271-272-273.

And lastly, **World Couriers of Queens** (718/978-9408) will send you, with hand-luggage, to London, Frankfurt, Milan or Zurich for only $200 round-trip if you book from four-to-six weeks in advance. A deal that can't be beat!

LET THEM EAT CAKE
287 Hudson Street
989-4970
American Express, MC, Visa
Closed Sunday, but orders taken around the clock

This is an example of a small store that sells primarily to department stores and restaurants but will gladly sell to you, too: Buy party cakes, sheet cakes, small cakes, and other sugar-coated delicacies at a fraction of what you'd pay elsewhere for the same item. Call for price quotes.

UNITED PARCEL SERVICE
695-7500
American Express, MC, Visa
Closed Saturday and Sunday

Unlike most other overnight and in-city delivery services, UPS has a sliding-scale fee system whereby they'll pick up at your door and deliver to another door for: $1.63 (within the city, next-day delivery); $9 (across the country, next-day); and up to $4 (second-day delivery up to a pound). These are extremely good rates, particularly since the mail in New York has slowed considerably. If you need a package delivered overnight in New York, UPS is the place to call.

THAT'S THE TICKET
718/375-4807

An "entertainment consultant" named Tommy sells

good seats at great prices for arena music and sporting events. Unlike the so-called scalpers, who would make you bald at the drop of a hat, this guy is legal and has a scale that includes moderate prices. Arena shows are $30–$45 and Tommy's rates are about 10 percent above for starters. The very expensive, or what he terms "outlandish and ridiculously good seats," can cost anywhere from $70 to $200. Call him before you wait outside on a rainy day. He will deliver tickets, too.

SUNGLASSES USA
469 Sunrise Highway, Lynbrook, New York 11563
800/USA-RAYS

This is the only place to buy Ray-Bans, or at least the only place I know of that you can possibly buy them if you are cost-conscious. Call for a catalogue, and find Classic Metals, Wayfarers, Upscales, Traditionals and Wings by Ray-Ban, and Bausch & Lomb. Prices are a nudge above wholesale. Ebony 22mm in gray are about $65–$70 in inexpensive shade stores. USA sells them for $38.50, plus $2 for shipping and handling. But you don't have to pay that. See coupon in the back.

LAND A-SALE!
Real Estate Department of the City of New York
2 Lafayette Street
806-8001
Auction held every two months

The city's real estate department holds land auctions every two months of plots and acreage that they don't want anymore. Often it comes from owners who haven't paid their taxes, and many of the plots are "minis": tiny, unusable pieces of city land in between two lots. (That's usually the fault of a surveyor who didn't measure right.) I've been told that people buy small pieces of land in New

York just in the hopes that some big corporation will need their plot and thus offer them a grand sum for their 50 feet! Write or call the department for information on buying up land, one investment that always seems to impress people.

CHAPTER 22

Novelties and Gift Items

Here's a list of places to go when you feel you need a gift to make a friend laugh or a small something to cheer yourself up.

THE FUNNY STORE OF MIDTOWN
1481 Broadway
730-9582

Times Square is home to one of the most important and least discussed tourist attractions in New York, and it's located right next door to Geraldo Rivera's T.V. studio. (For free tickets to his show, call 265-1283.) The Funny Store sells everything for the *gagster*. It's a novelty lover's paradise featuring hundreds of fakes: phony stains; powders that say "sugar" but produce solids when dropped in liquid; and fake fleas, cockroaches, and bees. They sell age-old jokes that never seem to grow tiresome, items that are advertised in the back pages of comic books!

I am told that if you are a practical joker, you will thrill to the racks of the Funny Store. But it also caters to the more immediate needs of New Yorkers and sells mace for protection (and photo I.D. cards, too). They have added a body condom to their stock for $14.98. "Why not be entirely safe?" the package ironically asks.

If you are a true novelty buff, you might want to see Merriment Boulevard, a nondescript strip of Broadway between 18th and 23rd Streets, where several wholesale and retail novelty shops hang their shingles, selling whoopee cushions, hand-shake buzzers, etc.

THE MAD MONK
500 Sixth Avenue
242-6678
American Express, MC, Visa

If you need a wedding present for some "hip" friends who haven't registered a pattern, you ought to come here. The shop is famous for classy pottery and colorful wall decorations; you can pay $10 for a clay-based key hanger you couldn't possibly buy anywhere else.

Monk calls itself "a museum of pottery," but I recommend shoppers venture into the back where novel gift items are sold. The sign that says "Please Touch" is a welcome attitude change from pottery stores that command you to be extra careful.

I can't believe how many $18–$20 vases and $15 wall sculptures Mad Monk stocks. When asked why prices were so low, a clerk smiled and suggested, "We charge what they're worth."

Check out (though not literally) the many shelves of books on diverse East-West philosophies, and see the racks with closeout specials in the back.

COME AGAIN
535 East 53rd Street
308-9394
American Express, MC, Visa
Closed Sunday

People who want sexual toys or erotic notions usually traipse to the West Village's infamous, and overpriced, **Pink Pussycat Boutique** (161 West Fourth Street, 243-0077, MC, Visa). Go to Come Again for a perfectly sane gift or necessity that relates to sex. The prices at this ten-year-old shop are about 15 percent lower than Pussycat's for oils, condoms (flavored, ribbed, or regular), sexual devices such as whips and chains, and even a full supply of phallic baked goods. (For the best in erotic cookies and cakes, try the sweets at **Erotic Baker,** 582 Amsterdam Avenue, 362-7557; American Express, MC, Visa; Closed Sunday.)

The best thing about Come Again is how much they differ from the shopkeepers at Pussycat. Here they have a keen sense of humor and, unlike the downtown store, don't treat their merchandise seriously. If you are curious about how to wear a rose-bud bikini—it comes rolled in plastic and fits 1/8 the normal body space—how to eat "edible panties," or how to use a set of benwa, feel free to discuss it with the staff.

You can purchase important literature and gadgets to help eroticize safer sex, including helpful overnight kits that start at $9.98 and are complete!

DAPY
431 West Broadway, 925-5082; 232 Columbus Avenue, 877-4710
American Express, MC, Visa

Not cheap. The gadgets stocked here are so colorful it doesn't matter that they are entirely pointless. Everything in the gift store is bright and zany—examples include neon telephones, speakers, televisions, and even neon-tone teapots.

They carry some "normal" products, too, but for those you can go to Macy's. I saw glassware and other usual gift items, such as wall plaques emblazoned with '50s diner waitresses. For those who need instant gratification, there's a Polaroid camera that takes the picture and places it on a wacky greeting card of your choice! They also have the best collection of loud wall clocks in town.

GAME SHOW
474 Sixth Avenue
633-6328
American Express, MC, Visa

Not cheap, part two. It was only a matter of time before a store filled with adult political and sexual board games came around to compete with *Wheel of Fortune.* Many of these pastimes concern illicit topics, such as How to Be a Bastard or the funny Fleece the Flock—a T.V. envangelist's game where a card instructs "Thou Shalt Not Cheat (unless thou canst get away with it)." People have a truly great time *in* this relaxed place. You can even buy educational games such as How to Be a Hollywood Producer. New York's cocktail party set has, at press time, warmly embraced Game Show.

There are even games for kids here, such as Anti-Monopoly, sure to please parents with faith in the Sherman Anti-Trust Act. "Politically-correct" toys for kids are best found at **Second Cousin** (142 Seventh Avenue South, 929-8048; American Express, MC, Visa), a store with class, also in the Village, that trades in concepts all parents would approve of.

WEST VILLAGE CONSIDERATIONS

♦ There is a certain corner downtown where several

streets intersect and where two stores with the same owner are filled with fun junk worth looking into: **Out of Our Drawers** (184 Seventh Avenue South, 929-4473; American Express, MC, Visa) sells specialty underwear ("Chutzpa Biker Pants") and *tschachkes* along the lines of bolo ties and wild earrings. The name means they sell anything they can get their hands on, used or new. "Ear Piercing—With or Without Pain" is the famous sign above this store, which you must be buzzed into through a locked gate.

♦ Across the street and catercorner, **Shades of the Village** (167 Seventh Avenue South, 255-7767) sells cheap *and* expensive varieties of sunglasses, in addition to crazy minutiae nobody needs. Just window shop. . . .

See coupon for both in the back.

♦ Next to Drawers is **Art Sanctuary,** a tourist attraction that sells odd and difficult-to-locate prints. Stock is featured on the sidewalk and inside a little hovel.

♦ Notable Village novelty: **Azuma** (25 East Eighth Street, 673-2900; American Express, MC, Visa) sells odd window shades, wicker furniture, mugs and vases, placemats, strange kitchen utensils, wholely unique sofa covers and bedspreads, and an assortment of gifts such as clocks, beads, and trunks.

BRASS LOFT
449 Broadway
226-5467
American Express, MC, Visa

One of the most interesting places to buy a gift, it is very difficult to go wrong at Brass Loft—even if you just want to spend $5. (See the next entry if you are willing to spend $10.) Brass Loft recently expanded and is now selling a greater variety of brass andirons, fireplace tools, hurricane lamps, animals in brass and copper, wall sconces, candlesticks and candelabras, chandeliers, planters, bar rails, and household accessories such as brass toilet-paper holders and kitchen racks.

At this store with the largest selection of brass giftware in the tri-state area, they sell with an effortless smile. Point being that even if it's something you truly do not need, it is a pleasure to buy here. They repair and repolish brass too.

See coupon in the back.

STRINGS
Locations all over Manhattan (new ones monthly)
967-5826
MC, Visa

Strings is a place to go for a small gift when you find that local card shops are just too expensive. Strings sells gifts for kids, adults, and seniors, all for just $10. The kids' gifts are charming—T-shirts, toys, and unusual ideas (remember the Whizzer Top?).

On those occasions when you don't want to bother with the local Hallmark, come to the store that has replaced the "69-Cent Shop." With inflation, $.69 has become $10, and Strings is still a blessing.

IMPORTANT ADVICE FOR NOVELTY BUFFS

If you haven't been to East 14th Street recently, you might be interested to know that the local Redevelopment Corporation that's descended on this shopping area has not been able to rid the block of good, atypical "variety stores." These are located at #108, #112, and #114 East

;; and as this book went to press, others were
... 14th Street's 100 block.

PEOPLE'S FLOWERS
786 Sixth Avenue
686-6291
MC, Visa

There is no flower you can't get for little money at
People's: a dozen carnations for $6, a gladiola for $1, silk
flowers for $1–$10 (depending on the texture), a cactus
for a few dollars. If you are making a bouquet, come to
People's.

If you like bonzais, try **Bonzai Store** (30th and Sixth,
no phone number; closed Sunday).

CHAPTER 23

Those Answered Questions

These pages comprise hard-earned pieces of information from years spent seeking bargains. Having taught classes on this subject as well, I can share some of the questions would-be bargain hunters have asked me, in hopes that they are your questions, too.

Q: Can I trust sidewalk salespeople?

A: Approach these vendors with suspicion—but don't ignore them. Sometimes you will discover that people simply enjoy vending on the street. But more likely than not, they do it because they can't afford a store, or have lost the lease on a shop.

The good thing is, street sellers hawk merchandise that you can touch: it's the what-you-see-is-what-you-get school of vending. But *never* buy anything shrink-wrapped (see chapter 4, "Flea Markets") because vendors have learned how to take old stuff and rewrap to make it look brand new.

Q: How come a chain like Lamston's Variety Store posts prices that vary widely from branch to branch?

A: When shopping, remember to use whatever sense of neighborhood you have: A Lamston's on the Upper East Side will be more expensive since they have to meet the demands of a higher rent than the 14th Street Lamston's. On West 23rd Street, where Lamston's has been located since before the area was gentrified, the rent is much cheaper, as are the pricetags.

Q: You talk about chain stores a lot; please tell me why you think they're deceiving.

A: First, chain stores usually sell merchandise at regular price—a little below "list price." Chain boutiques often look like they are discount outlets; they're not. For women, the chain Conway's on East 34th Street is the exception to the rule. Most important, chain store *names* are deceiving. For example, Sock Express and New York Sock Mart sound alike and even look similar. However, Express sells $7 pairs of athletic white socks while the Sock Mart offers two pairs for the same price. (The latter is, incidentally, at 79 Chambers Street, 766-2068.)

Q: Fashion, where are you?

A: Mind these fashion notes: Artful fashion is everywhere, but you have to be on the lookout for it. Make friends with the sales help at fine stores; likely then they will always take a phone call from you, they may clue you in about private sales, and they may even put something aside for you. Go, look, come back. Clerks like careful shoppers. . . . Try to have an idea of what you're looking for; then the salesperson will be willing to help for as long as you need. Follow seasonal advice—buy off-season merchandise as much as you can.

Q: Why all this talk about seasons?

A: Understanding seasons is essential for the bargain hunter. The seasons in the fashion world are known as Spring, Fall, Transition, and Holiday. Spring starts right after real-time spring begins, and the rest of the seasons follow suit. (All except Holiday, which begins in late Fall.) But don't shop at the beginning or in the middle of a season. Wait until the end, when people are trying to clear the racks at high speed! And that's the best time to visit a department store.

Q: What's the best month to go shopping?

A: August—or anytime in late summer.

Q: The worst is December, right?

A: Not necessarily. (Though, to be frank, you'd be smart if you attempted to get your Christmas shopping out of the way during the pre-Christmas sale days in November. Or better yet, shop for gifts in March when sales on winter items occur.) December is a madhouse, true, but there are blissful late afternoons before hordes of shoppers descend onto the streets. At about 3 p.m. on any December weekday, wander into any store and peacefully enjoy various last-minute "shopping bonuses" to help you save money.

Q: How is it you compare shopping in department stores to shopping in supermarkets?

A: Shopping at a department store should be seen in the same manner as shopping at a supermarket. When you go into a supermarket, never buy what's straight ahead of your eye: those are the high-end, heavily advertised products. Instead, if you look down or up, you will see bargain products or the no-name brands.

Likewise, at a department store you should never buy the clothing right off the aisle, because that's the most accessible merchandise and it's usually the very expensive stocks. If you wander through to the back, you will see bins and off-rack items that at one time stood in that privileged position off the aisle. And now their prices have dropped considerably. (There are closeouts in nearly every section of a department store! See Introduction.)

Q: What about bin-shopping?

A: Bins are places where clothing and other merchandise is folded and not hung up. In many instances this is your lucky place to shop. Things taken off hangers are placed in bins and are cheaper. You'll have to do some ironing.

Q: Where's the best matzoh ball soup in New York?

A: In my opinion, the heartiest matzohs are at Bernstein's, the city's only Chinese/Jewish diner (135 Essex Street, 473-3900).

Q: How do I go about getting Broadway and Off-Broadway tickets on the cheap?

A: Here are two ways. Write to the Theater Development Fund (TDF) at 1501 Broadway, New York, NY 10036 (221-0885). Send them $15 and they'll send you vouchers worth $5 or more for tickets at new and long-running Off-Broadway shows. In addition, as a member of TDF, you are offered two $8–$12 tickets to Broadway and Off-Broadway shows.

TDF also runs the famed "TKTS" booths, which were recently redesigned for quicker service. These booths are located, in Manhattan, at Duffy Square, 47th Street and Broadway, and 2 World Trade Center; in Brooklyn, at locations in Brooklyn Heights and Williamsburg. The ticket booths sell day-of-show tickets for half price (at the World Trade Center you can buy weekend tickets on Friday) plus a $1.75 charge service.

The second thing to do is send a self-addressed stamped envelope to the Hit Show Club, the people who manufacture and distribute "twofer" coupons that are redeemable at the box office for 1/3-off nearly any Broadway show. Hit Show gives away "twofers" at their office, too, at 630 Ninth Avenue (581-4211). (The expiration date on the "twofer" is for the last show date you can use the coupon for, not the last day on which you can buy tickets.)

Q: What does the term "previous markdown" mean?

A: Often you'll see a line in a sales circular or advertisement that says, "There have been previous markdowns."

All that means is this is a unique promotion b
you might have seen a better price at that store on u.
item at an earlier date.

Q: How can I avoid being taken advantage of?

A: Simply never appear desperate. And, again, take your
time.

Q: What's the most used name in retail?

A: For some reason, a different store with the monicker
"Vogue" pops up at regular intervals. Who knows, maybe
store owners think that the public is gullible enough to
imagine that *Vogue* magazine runs the shop.

Q: Public bathrooms are a problem—any suggestions?

A: Except for grungy bathrooms in the subways, no. But
I have one friend who is always out and about; her trick
is to say to a restaurant or cafe owner, "If I ask you nicely,
can I use your bathroom?" No one has ever turned down
that straightforward approach!

Q: You hardly mention Canal Street—why?

A: Canal, one of New York's two-way shopping thor-
oughfares, is a legendary street; earlier in the decade many
of the city's brothels were located on this block. If you
compare the old Canal Street to the new, not much has
really changed. Now, though, it's overflowing with junk
shops and very unfriendly vendors. (The electronic store
Uncle Steve's has unfriendly service and bargains galore;
see chapter 20, "Home Appliances.")

Q: Why do many people consider bargain hunting rude,
unnecessary, or a complete waste of time?

A: Those people haven't learned one thing my family
instilled in me: that money is pretty much irretrievable.
To me, taking the time to hunt out a bargain is always
worthwhile, especially when you can be proud of what
you bought, *and* proud of how little money was doled out.

Q: What's "whim shopping"?

A: Whim shopping is buying on impulse. Some people
call this "spec shopping" because, though you buy it, you

aren't sure it's right for you. Often whim shoppers find themselves rationalizing a good buy with, "I don't need this, but I'm buying it anyway." If this is an inexpensive item, fine. But bargain hunters, beware—this could be your nemesis.

Q: I, Michael on the Upper East Side allegedly sells Jackie O's hand-me-downs—is he for real?

A: Michael is neat, and he's got terrific women's bargains on gowns. See chapter 11, "Outerwear."

Q: What will I find at the traveling Greenmarkets that's truly cheap?

A: Wine, bread, muffins, flowers, some apples (some are expensive but delicious), and more. Call 556-0990 to see where these outdoor markets are in any given week.

Q: I saw a store on 49th Street and Seventh Avenue that was actually called "Closeout!" What was that all about?

A: Just like those outfits that constantly advertise "Going out of Business" (GOOB), these are stores that want you to believe they are turning over stock every day. The difference between closeout shops and GOOB operations is that often closeouts are really getting rid of tons of merchandise at outlandishly low prices. The GOOB boutiques are 100 percent gimmick.

Q: How do some fur shops hawk inexpensive furs all year round when fur is supposed to be cut-rate only in the summer?

A: Harry Kirschner and Sons (307 Seventh Avenue, 243-4847) sells furs at about 50 percent below retail year round. They figure it this way: The fur season doesn't get into high gear until late summertime, so they keep stock turning from late summer until the following spring. That way they always have a sale going on. Essentially, they never put all their stock on display at one time. See chapter 11, "Outerwear."

Q: Are there neighborhoods I should avoid?

A: No. But I will qualify my views on midtown Manhattan since I do talk about it a lot. This isn't the safest area to shop in. Be extra careful. Don't be flamboyant with your cash. Don't shop alone. Don't give out your credit card number (someone could use it to charge things over the telephone) and if you use a card, be sure to get your carbons back. Don't ever volunteer personal information on a credit card slip—a 1989 New York law states you do not have to give a phone number or address when charging. And don't make it known that you don't regularly shop in the neighborhood.

Q: What's the benefit of getting chummy with clerks?

A: Particularly in the districts—see chapter 2, "Comprehending the Districts"—you should encourage a friendly sales clerk. This way, in areas where everyone sells something you're interested in, you will be privvy to insiders' information: who's moved in, who's moved out, who's closing their stock, who's disreputable. Also, when you're friendly you are treated like a friend. And friends don't want you to waste your money.

Q: Why do I get the feeling Fifth Avenue is very expensive?

A: Because it is. Once a year, though, around Christmas time, everyone drops their prices just a little. And Fifth Avenue turns into a Winter Wonderland Mall on the second Sunday of December: that's when you can shop your heart out, eat, listen to music, watch magicians, and have a merry time. All the traffic is rerouted.

Q: You talk about warehouse sales; what's the best one?

A: It happens once a year, when Barney's, the pricey men's and women's store with a warehouse at 243 West 17th Street (929-9000), has its annual sale. During this week-long event, dressed-up folks line up for blocks to see Barney's normally bankrupting prices become almost affordable.

Q: What's the secret of mailing lists?

A: Ask twice if you must, but just make sure you're on the mailing list of the stores that intrigue you. You get invited to private sales, you find out about "sneak previews" before the public, and you get wonderful coupons in the mail.

Q: Is there a sneaky way to find out in advance about the big sample sales held in midtown?

A: Call Accurate Distribution, who prints and distributes notices posted and handed out around town (766-1900).

Q: Do "wholesale only" shops still exist?

A: At one time it was an advantage for an establishment to limit itself to wholesale; wholesalers could avoid heavy tax burdens. So even today, a vendor will often refuse to sell retail if he hasn't discovered the newly instituted tax advantages of selling to everyone. But in most cases—particularly in shops from West 23rd to West 29th Streets just off Broadway—you will find that "wholesale only" places will sell to individuals who ask them, "Please?"

Q: How can I know which mail order houses to trust?

A: Only buy from people whom you can get in touch with quickly. That is, make sure they have an 800 number or some phone number with which you can check up on them. Try to get the office number instead of a customer service number.

Q: How can I be sure not to get ripped off via mail order?

A: Remember to inspect all merchandise for general defects and accuracy of order the very minute the package arrives. Before you pay in full, follow these rules for shopping by mail: Make sure they tell you how long it will take to get to you; ask how valuable or vulnerable merchandise will be shipped; and insure those valuables.

Q: Is there one piece of definitive advice you can give the bargain hunter?

A: *Never hurry your selection.* Go slow. You can go back for it, and if you can't, it probably was not meant to be yours.

Q: There must be another piece of advice you've left out?

A: If you want something and aren't sure if the price is right, ask the vendor if he is "sure" that's the going rate on the item. You'd be surprised how many sellers will drop the price a little to get you to buy. Note well: it's always a buyer's market.

Q: If you had one place to shop in, which would it be?

A: I'd have to choose two: Since I always shop for clothing and CDs, find me at the Manhattan Century 21 (12 Cortlandt Street, 227-9092) where I can find outerwear, underwear, face cream, toothpaste, socks, and much more (see chapters 8 and 11); and Record World in Queens (70-34 Austin Street (718/263-8625). That particular Record World is located in Forest Hills, where I was born. And I'm sentimental.

CHAPTER 24

Transitional Blocks

This chapter and the next are meant for the ultimate bargain shoppers, and provide extra information for those who have studied up on the preceding information and are now ready for bonuses. Enjoy these two chapters for extra special bargains and remember: a bargain is a bargain only if you buy it on your own terms.

EIGHTH AVENUE IN MIDTOWN
From 23rd to 40th Street

This is where the fun begins for adventurous shoppers: **Parts Unlimited** (#274), down on Eighth Avenue and West 24th Street, has good deals on small electronic devices and replacement parts, but (amazing) free estimates on *any repair*. In a 1987 study for a national magazine, I compared the prices of T.V. repair shops, and

Parts Unlimited was the absolute lowest in town. There are dozens of hardware stores along this strip, too.

On Eighth in the low 30s you will find off-price garment centers selling T-shirts, jeans, jackets, and assorted accessories. (These places have strange names such as **Jackie's, Poco Poco, Poppins,** and **Robbins;** the latter has good prices on no-brand undergarments.) Also, see **Ceway** (#496) for cheap computer hardware; **Sakhi Fabrics** (#580) for sewing equipment; and **Kiuto Bakery,** (#405) the original sellers of the Baby Watson Cheesecake.

CHAMBERS STREET
Between Church Street and Broadway

This neck of Chambers is soon to be turned into co-op heaven; meanwhile, it's an area that is so underused it has induced area landlords to allow low-rent or no-rent "warehouse stores." I walked into an outlet marked with that name and found Neutrogena Shampoo, normally retailing at about $5, on sale at a tax-free $1.20! When I asked how come it was so cheap, the clerk shrugged, "It's a sale."

This is very good news for consumers: these stores sell just about everything—from books to cosmetics—and apparently below cost. The proprietors have almost no overhead and usually buy in bulk.

I suggest you go on a Saturday when the workaday crowd is at home. Buy books, linens, jewels, slightly damaged clothing, and hardware at a "hardware store" that sells everything from burglar alarms to toilet seats. Other Chamber ideas include **Mashuguna Ike** (#111), a Crazy Eddie-type stereo store whose slogan is "I will not lose a sale!" and **Chocolate Factory,** an amazing nosh hangout (#93).

What I love about Chambers is that nearly every month a new store takes a chance on it. For instance, at press time the **Fellini Florsheim** shoe store (#86)—with hard-to-locate men's quality footwear—had a splashy opening with a "half off" sale on everything, a sale they keep repeating in local papers. But Chambers is changing and it will soon be nothing but a memory.

ANOTHER SIDE OF 14TH STREET
Between Sixth and Ninth Avenues

There are two stretches of 14th Street that seem to be on their way up. The first is 14th Street off of Sixth Avenue, with a series of large clothing stores using names like **Bunnie's For Children, Bazaar Shops,** and **We Sell Whole Sale.** All of these have opened up in defunct department stores or boutiques. Then, from Seventh Avenue on, there are bookstores, an excellent Korean restaurant (#248), "underground" Spanish restaurants, a family shoe store called **John's** (#204) with great prices, and several Spanish dry goods stores filled with refrigerated delicacies. Also find a store dedicated to cheap vacuum cleaners called **Desco** (#131), and **A to Z** (#139), one of the best stocking-up stores for cosmetics and bathroom goods. While you're there, see various video and music stores with a large selection of ethnic tapes, CDs, and even records. For more on 14th Street, see chapter 25, "Unnoticed Areas."

WARREN STREET
Between Church Street and Broadway

In this short stretch of Warren you will locate a women's clothing outlet called **Damages** and a variety of good kick-around shoe stores for women (one is actually called **Lady Diana**). You must see the **Fountain Pen Hospital** for a great selection of stationery goods, and stores that include a pet shop, a plant shop, and a shop for quality briefcases. Get printed invitations at **Phillipson-Chamberts Press,** and try **Finesse** for small appliances.

Best bet: Stop at the only soul food restaurant for miles—**Ham Heaven**—and then make a quick turn onto Church Street to find the original **Pushcart Job Lot** store, a monster filled with items ranging from cheap stationery to fine colognes, all trucked in daily (see chapter 4, "Flea Markets"). You will also see stores that may not look that reputable, but give good deals on leather bags, vitamins, coffee, books from Ireland, razors, and a host of electronics accessories, such as batteries, audio and video cassettes, and photographic equipment.

CHAPTER 25

Unnoticed Areas

UPPER MADISON AVENUE
Between 86th and 96th Streets

This chapter covers unadvertised places in unfamiliar parts of Manhattan. What you will find on Madison Avenue in the 80 and 90 blocks is truly amazing. There are jewelry specialty shops, engraving and print marts, and even a **Soldier Shop** for war memories (#1222). As you head up Madison from 86th Street note how the number of boutiques drops as croissants make their appearance and "Charming Breakfast Specials" are advertised for $10! But at #1227 find Manhattan's only branch of local delicatessen, **Petak's,** a real Jewish grocery store that is even better than Zabar's because it's stocked with truly hard-to-find delicacies. Then see places like **90th Street Pharmacy,** an old-fashioned drug store that has been in the family since 1890, and offers good service and products—a lesson for vendors on longevity.

At about 94th Street, on the bottom of the hill, you start to see chain stores such as **Fotomat** film processors, and **K & D Wines,** an authentic "wine factory outlet" with sale prices every day. Ancient stamp machines and ladies mending shirts in the window lend the impression of a small village; camera repairs and cheap grocery stores now appear. The spruced-up streets in this part of town have won community contests for beautiful gardens.

FIRST AVENUE IN THE EAST VILLAGE
Between St. Marks Place and Houston Street

Refrigerators, air conditioners, and cheap antique clothing are what makes the East Village's First Avenue a spectacular shopping attraction. **J. Eis and Son** (#107) and **Bloom and Klup** (#228) still sell used refrigerators— new ones, too—and feature stoves, ovens, floor fans, and microwaves. In the old days you could look up to the second floor on First Avenue and see scores of second-hand ovens and refrigerators. Today you're more likely to see a gallery, club, or macrobiotic restaurant.

14TH STREET PROPER
Between Broadway and Sixth Avenue

Everything can be found on 14th, just take a look on a tour that goes west from Broadway: start below the boulevard at **Cheap Jack's,** an antique clothing mart that is a veteran of the buy-one-get-one-free methodology. Broadway has **America,** a chain store that screams its "Bah-Gahns" on a megaphone all day long. Across the street is **Seaman's,** an ordinary furniture store with closeouts every week. (Chain stores on 14th have lower overhead, therefore they usually have lower prices, than anywhere else in town.)

Paterson's Silk at University Place is the only custom reupholstery place downtown. A little further west, **Grand Discount** has 14th Street's only sincere seven-day return policy. And **Petland Discount** indeed has a small selection, but it's an entertaining stopover during a long shopping spree.

Chains here include **Thom McAn** and **Fayva** shoe stores, **Woolworth, Savemart** and **Trader Horn** for small appliances, T.V.s, stereo units, and microwaves. Trader Horn always has a "loss-leader" color T.V. that they sell for around $100; they advertise this in hopes of getting you to the store. And a little further down is **Robbins,** a wholesale distributor advertising a vague "6 to 60 percent" off all merchandise. They sell sheets, towels, unstylish jeans, T-shirts, and household goods. People swear by this fluorescent wonderland; to me, it means rustling through bins stocked so high you can't possibly get through to the bottom.

More important than these particulars, however, is the essence of 14th Street. If you can put up with the hawkers who have no shame—they will sit on ladders in the middle of the sidewalk and use bullhorns—you can buy from reputable dealers which do exist regardless of what redevelopers say. Limit shopping on 14th Street to household appliances and cleaners—things like towels, kitchen goods, and Walkmans—and you'll do fine. Interestingly, many stores offer return guarantees of *cash;* so don't bother with those who don't (**Jack's** and **Jay's Bargains** are two places with firm no-return policies).

The block is dotted with junk shops that can be a great source of inspiration. You might end up saying, "I really can use that!" See **Vim** for jeans and cheap sneakers; **Camptown Army-Navy** for great sales of 501s and army-navy supplies, but not great service; and **14th Street Hi-Fi** for bargain basement prices on stereo speakers and portable CD players.

For more on 14th Street, see chapter 24, "Transitional Blocks."

BROADWAY IN SOHO
Broadway between Houston Street and Spring Street

Here you are—savings headquarters for the adventurous. You can find lingeries, shoes, linens, and other bargains and markdowns at mainly Hispanic-owned factory warehouse outlets. Yes, the tarot card readers are still here, but unlike the rest of Soho, only a couple of stores are expensive.

Up until the mid-1980s, these places, even the minimart at Prince, sold exclusively wholesale. Now that tax laws have relaxed—they can sell to anyone. Spend time going store to store, seeing what fabrics or ancient fashion ideas (**Fashion Hats**, 579 Broadway) you might run across. Try **Soho Surplus** (594), a trendy army-navy store with old price tags. Right above Houston is **National Liquidators Warehouse** (632), an aesthetically pleasing shop with stationery, kitchenware, *tschachkes,* even cheap art!

Below Houston on Broadway you'll find, for example, Korean textile places, famous menswear stop **Mano a Mano,** and other casual men's clothing stores flanking it. Also, #575 is an address to keep in mind: the owners keep changing but they continue to sell well-priced jeans. **Ben Raymond Fabric** at #623 will sell you "anything you want" in a trimming.

This is not a well-recognized shopping area; when people go to Soho, they usually shop along West Broadway, the boulevard a few blocks west of Broadway. But now you know better: the real bargains are on the real Broadway.

LOWER FIFTH AVENUE
Between 33rd and 14th Streets

Few shoppers bother with the southern tip of Fifth because they believe that lower Fifth Avenue, below 34th Street and the defunct B. Altman's, has nothing but schlock shops and delicatessens.

True, there are plenty of that ilk. But there are also plenty of places that you should try—only on weekdays—for good showroom and warehouse sales. Some of these are much lower than 34th Street, in the teens and twenties along Fifth Avenue. Look into these buildings: #85 has menswear outlets; #115 is home to **Lesh,** one of the old-fashioned menswear outfitters; #123 houses factory showrooms; #200 has an assortment of clothiers for men and women—sportswear, activewear, and formal wear. Go into the lobbies and read listings on the wall.

Many fine tailors are situated along Fifth Avenue, including **Murray Waxman** at #85. You will see such great stores as **Brownies** at #91, a store with everything for the naturalist (food, vitamins, books, lotions). See **Weissman-Heller & Sons** at #129 for everyday sample sales on modern furniture pieces (see chapter 3, "Sample Sales"). Also on Fifth are scuba stores, hobby stores surrounding the **Toy Center** (northwest corner of 23rd Street and Fifth) record shops, and very inexpensive stereo outlets. One of the stereo stops, indubitably worth a visit, is **Joy-Lud Electronics** from the Soviet Union, who, thanks to perestroika, can sell goods to Russian citizens and others. Their stock includes an ancient answering machine and hi-fi units. Everything is displayed right out of the box.

Little India is located along this stretch of Fifth. Find specialty cold cuts, lace and linen shops, and at 30th Street, a place that has both in its window and stockroom dozens of old-fashioned bedspreads. **Nader Foods** at #256 is a perfect site to learn about Indian culture, with small prices for authentic spices, sweets, and delicacies.

Find a pretty sari at #296. At the corner of 33rd Street are inexpensive costume jewelry shops that have been around for decades. The shopkeepers there will always haggle.

ACKNOWLEDGMENTS

I would like to thank these people for their help in making *Bargain Hunting in Greater New York* a reality: Jeff Herman, Karen Romer, Robin Lockwood, Amy Pattullo, Ilene Diamond, Elysa Lazar, Adam Sternbach, Jeanine Moss, Jonathan Herzog, David Rothenberg, Ryoko Sawaishi, Ricardo Matamoros, Jim Philipps, Laurence Lerman, Suki M. John, Jennifer Leigh Warren, Charles Paikert, Matthew and Emily Laermer, David Morgenstern, and a collection of vendors and knowledgeable tri-state residents who colluded with me to let others in on the real "cheapos." Thank you to Rachel Kranz for her moral and other support; Natalie Atlas Unger for taking the time to proofread every word; to Randy Matusow for her ten-million-dollar photos, and to the Learning Annex—who forced me to research bargains in the first place—and the students who reinforced my belief that everyone loves what my grandmother calls "metsieh."

Thanks to Ben Dominitz, Laura Glassover, Jennifer Basye, and Nancy Martinelli for their continued support of both *Bargain Hunting* and *Native's Guide to New York*.

A

AACA Craftsfair, 28–29
A & M Furs, 75
Aaron's, 95
ABC Carpet, 148
Abe Geller, 79, 96
Abraham & Straus (A&S), xii
  carpet cleaning, 150
Abraham & Straus (A&S)
  (Brooklyn), xii, 59–60
Abraham & Straus (A&S)
  (Queens), xii
Accessories Arcade, 8
Accessories Plus, 40
Accurate Distribution, 192
Ace Leather, 138–139
Addidas, 39
Address chart of Manhattan,
  xiii–xiv
Adorama, 161–162
Adrienne Jewelry Specialists, 121
Aida's & Jim's Merchandising
  Company, 22, 106
Aida's & Jimi's Merchandising
  Company, 106
Aileen Factory Outlet, 71
Alexanders, xii
Alexanders (Bronx; Brooklyn), xii
Alice's Wonderland, 69
Alice Underground, 11, 87
All-in-One, 42
All Ireland Irish Import Store,
  57–58
Altman Luggage, 136–137
Amazing Foods, 129–130
America, 199
American Museum of Natural
  History, 122
American Tourister, 70, 141–142
Ananias, 140

Anne Klein Outlet
  Flemington, 44
  Woodbury Common, 70
Annex Antiques Fair, 23–24, 25
Antique Boutique, 94
Antique clothing. See Second-hand
  clothing
Antique/Craft Show at Holy Cross
  High School, 28
Antiques
  districts for, 12
  flea markets, 23–24
Antiques at Dale's, 51–52
Apparel Connection, 39
Apparel. See Clothing
Appliances. See Home appliances
Archie McPhee and Company, 7
Arena Liquidators, 130
Arise Furniture Warehouse, 151
Art Sanctuary, 182
A. Rubenstein & Sons, 83–84
Astor Place Hair Designers, 114–115
Athlete's Foot, 2, 6–7
Athletic Outlet, 69
A to Z Discounts, 116–117, 196
A To Z Luggage, 137–138
Auctions, 27–28
  federal surplus goods, 173
  Police Department Auctions, 27
  Post Office Auctions, 27
Avery Book Store, 66–67
Avirex Factory, 20–21
Azuma, 182

B

Bag House, The, 140–141
Bagmakers Factory Store, 44
Bali Factory Outlet, 39
Bally, 40
Barbara Gee Dancewear, 102

Barbizon Lingerie, 40
Barclay School Supplies, 65–66
Barnes & Nobles, 15
Barney's, xii, 191
Bass Shoe Factory Outlet
  Harmon Cove Outlet Center, 40
  Woodbury Common, 69
Bathrooms, public, 189
Battery Park Crafts Show, 24–25
Bazaar Shops, 196
Beautiful Visions USA LTD, 110
Beauty Boutique, 118
Beauty Scenter, 44
Beauty Showcase, 111
Beckenstein Fabrics, 48
Beckenstein's Ladies Fabric, 48
Bendel's, xii
Ben Farber's, 95–96
Ben Raymond Fabric, 201
Bergdorf Goodman, xii
Berkeley's, 115
Bernies Discount Center, 163
Bernsteins, 188
Ber-Sel Handbags, 137
Be Seated Inc., 151–152
Bianco's, 124
Binkin's Book Store, 66
Bin-shopping, 187–188
Bi-Rite Photo and Electronics,
  164–165
Bloom and Klup, 199
Bloomingdale's, xii
  carpet cleaning, 150
Bloomingdale's By Mail, 35
Body Shop, The, 119
Bogie's Antique Furs and Clothing, 80
Bon Marche, 148
Bonzai Store, 184
Books, districts for, 14
Boot Town Warehouse Outlet, 36
Brass Loft, 182–183
Broadway in Soho, 201
Broadway Panhandler, 132
Brooklyn, 51–58, 59–67
  Flatbush, 59–67
  lighting, 151
Brooklyn Botanic Garden, 173
Brownies, 202
Bryant Park Crafts Show, 24–25
Bucci, 42
Bunnie's For Children, 196
Burlington, New Jersey, 42
Burlington Bag & Baggage, 37
Burlington Coat Factory, 42
Burlington Mart, 43

C

Calvin Klein outlets
  Enterprise Avenue, 41
  Liberty Village, 44
  Secaucus, 39
Camptown Army-Navy, 200–201
Canal Jeans, 84–85, 94
Canal Self Service Store, 131
Canal Street, 189
Canal Street Flea Market, 24
Cancer Care Thrift Shop, 99
Capezio Shoe Outlet, 42, 101–102
Carlsen Import, 4
Carnegie Luggage, 139
Carpet Fashions, 149
Carpeting, 148–150
Carter's Childrenswear, 69
Cartier, 120
Castle Road Outlet Center, 38–39
CDs, districts for, 9–10
Central Carpeting, 149
Century 21 Department Stores, 57,
  78–79, 193
Ceway, 195
Chain stores, 186
Chambers Street, 195–196
Chandlers, 2–3
Chang's Gallery, 170
Charles S. Cohen & Sons, 8
Cheap Jack's, 88, 199
Chelsea Frames, 170
Children's Outlet, 40
Children's wear, 40, 104–109
  sample sales, 22
China, Glass, and Gift Outlet, 41
Chocolate Factory, 195
Chocolate Soup, The, 138
Choice Seating, 153–154
Christie's, 27
Christie's East, 28
Christine Valmy School, 114
Church's English Shoe Shop, 39
City Athlete, The, 8
City Dump, 26
Clairol Consumer Research Center,
  116
Clairol Test Center, 116
Clay Pot, The, 134–135
Clearance, ix
Closeout, ix
Clothes Works, 72
Clothing, size charts, xiv–xv
Colognes. *See* Perfumes
Colonial Sportshoe Center, 72
Come Again, 180

Competitive Edge Fitness, 114
Complete Collegiate, Inc., The,
171–172
Computers, 156–167
Conran's, 146–147
Consumer Information Center, 167
Conway's, 186
Cooper-Hewitt Museum, 122
Corning, Connecticut, 73
Corning Factory Store, 69, 73
Corning Glass Works Factory, 73
Corning Ware outlet, 44
Cosmetics, 110–119
Cosmetics Plus, 118
Couriers, 170–171
  air couriers, 174
Current, Inc., 35
Curtis Furniture Company, 147–148
Cusom furniture, 153–154
Custom Furniture Factory Outlet,
153

D

DAC Lighting Manufacturing,
150–151
Daffy Don's, 100–101
Damages, 94–95, 196
Dance & Music Hotline, 173
D & A Merchandise, 50
Dan Klemuk's Gazebo, 152
Dansk Factory Outlet
  Flemington, 43
  Woodbury Common, 70
Danson Jewelers, 39
Dapy, 180–181
DAT'S Incredible, 162
Dave's Army & Navy Store, 82
December shopping, 187
Dembitzer Brothers, 159–160
Department of Defense Auctions,
173
Department stores, 187
  list of, xi–xiii
  season price break at, xi
Desco Appliance, 163
Designer Apparel Mart, 49
Designer Luggage Depot, 40
Design Furniture International
  Showroom, 152
Destino, Ralph, 29
Detail, 126
Deutsch Inc., 152
Dial A Contact Lens, 36–37
Dial-a-Dinner, 174
Dial-A-Mattress, 32
Diamond Masquerade, 39

Diamonds by Rennie Ellen, 123
Diners, 10
Discount Couriers, 170–171
Districts, 9–16
  clerks in, 191
  for jewelry, 120–121
Doe-Spun outlet, 44
Dollar Bill's, 86–87
Door Store, 146–147
Drugstores, districts for, 10
Dunham, 2

E

E & B Discount Marine, 34
East 33rd Typwriter and Elec-
  tronics, 165
East Vincent Luggage Shop, 141
East Village, First Avenue in, 199
Easy address chart of Manhattan,
  xiii–xiv
E.B.A. Wholesalers, 64
Eighth Avenue in Midtown,
  194–195
Eisner Brothers, 86
Ekkon, 196
Eklektic Designer Dreams, 70
Eldridge Textile Company, 32–33
Electronics, 156–167
Elite Shoe Repair, 140
Encore-Resale Dress Shop, 99
Enterprise Avenue, 41
Erotic Baker, 180
Erotic goods, 180
Essential Products, 113
Essex Umbrella Corporation, 134
Europa, 46
Euro-Tire, 32
Everybody's Thrift Shop, 88
  Exchange Unlimited, 88
Exclusively Yours Personal Trainers,
  114
Executive Apparel, 19
Executive Neckwear, 40
Exotic Fragrances, 112
Extended warranty plans, 166–167
Extra protection plans, 166–167
Eyewear
  mail-order, 36–37
  sample sales, 22

F

Fabric Alternative, 52–53
Fabrics, districts for, 14
Fashion Flair, 40
Fashion Hats, 201
Faxes, 164–165

Faxes, 164–165
Faxland, 165
Fayva, 200
Federal surplus goods, 173
Fellini Florsheim, 195–196
Fellman Ltd., 1
Fenn Wright & Manson, 19
Fenwick Clothes, 90
Fieldcrest Cannon Factory Outlet, 73
Fifth Avenue, 191
    Lower, 202–203
Fine & Klein, 47–48
Finesse, 196
Fin Fur, 75
First Avenue in East Village, 199
Fish markets, 14
Flatbush, 59–67
Flatiron District, 13
Flea markets, 23–29
    in Connecticut, 28
Flemington, New Jersey, 43–44
Flemington Traffic Circle, 43
Flemington's Liberty Village, 43
Flowers. *See* Plants and flowers
Foods, 129–130
Forcellini, 42
Foremost Furniture, 144
Forman's, 49
Fortunoff's, 120
47th Street Photo, 167
Foto Cell, 30
Foto Electric Supply Company, 156–157
Fotomat, 199
Fountain Pen Hospital, 131–132, 196
14th Street
    another side of, 196
    proper, 199–200
14th Street Hi-Fi, 201
Fowad, 85–86
Frankel's Discount Store (For Boots), 55
Frank's, 115
Freeda Vitamins, 132–133
Friedlich Inc., 45–46
Fulton Market, 14
Funky clothing stores, 15
Funny Store of Midtown, The, 178–179
Furniture, 143–155. *see also* Antiques
    custom furniture, 153–154
    flea markets, 23–24
    phone services, 154
Furniture Distributors of America, 154

Furniture Sales, 24
Furs, 74–80, 190
    districts for, 10–11
    sample sales, 21
Futon Flow, 151
Futons, 151

G

Game Show, 181
G & B Sneaker Center, 8
G & J Art Pieces, 43
Gap for Kids, The, 109
Garment center, 13–14
Gemini Paper Goods, 129
Gem Pawnbrokers, 61
Gene London Productions, 79
General Services Auction, 173
Geraldo Rivera's show, 178
GGMC Parking, 171
Gifts, 127–135, 178–184
Giftwarehouse Outlet, 39
Gilcrest-Townsman Clothes Co., 89–90
Giorgiolini, 8
Gitano Factory Store, 40–41
Glass Factory Outlet, 72
Glemby International, 116
Gloria Umbrella Manufacturing Company, 134
GMC Garage Management, 171
Going out of business sale, ix
Goldin Feldman Furs, 21, 76
Goldman and Cohen, 49
Good junk districts, 14
Gourmet Basket, 70
Grand Discount, 200
Greater New York Trading Company, 135
Greenmarkets, 190
Grieco's Car Rental, 170
Grieco's Van Rental, 170

H

Haircuts
    cheap cuts, 114–115
    freebies, 115–116
Halbart Air Service, 174–175
Ham Heaven, 197
Hamilton Factory, 44
Hamilton Watch Factory, 69
Hanae Mori, 134
Handbags, 136–142
    districts for, 12
    mail-order, 37
Hanes, 39
Harmon Cove Outlet Center, 40–41

Harold Reuter Foreign Exchange, 169
Harris Levy Importers, 33
Harry Kirschner and Sons, 76, 190
Harvé Benard
    Latham Outlet Village, 71–72
    Woodbury Common, 69
Hats for men, 91–92
Headlines, 173
Hilton Manufacturing Company, 21
Hit Show Club, 188
Home appliances, 156–167
    districts for, 12–13
Home Fabric Store, 48
Home Sales, 154
Home Sales Dial-A-Discount, 164
Hot Shoes, 7
Household items, 127–135. *see also*
    Home appliances
Hudson's, 82

I

Ikea, 144–145
I, Michael, 78, 99, 190
Indian Museum, 123
International Jewelry Mart, 121
International Leather Expo,
    The, 153
Intimate Eve, 41

J

Jackies, 195
Jack's, 200
James Roy, 154
J & H Katz, 8
J & R Music World, 31, 166
Jay's Bargains, 200
Jay's Perfume Bar, 111
J. Crew Catalogue, 1002–103
Jean-Pierre Sand Skin Care, 113
J. Eis and Son, 199
Jeff Jacobs Flea Market, 28
Jensen-Lewis Co., 145–146
Jerry's Job Lot, 111, 135
Jewelry, 120–126
    districts for, 12
    sample sales, 20
Jewish food and artifacts, 15
Jewish Museum, 123
Jindo Furs, 74–75
J.J. Hat Shop, 91–92
Joan & David, 44
John Atchison, 116
John Cipriano, 8
John's, 196
John's Shoe Store, 4–5

Jolie Madame, 8
Jone Schifrin, 20
Joy-Lud Electronics, 162, 202

K

K & D Wines, 199
Kidstuff Factory Outlet, 39
Kiehls, 119
King Arthur's Liquidation Center,
    130
Kingsway Video, 162
Kirk's Folly, 123
Kitchen Place, 43
Kiuto Bakery, 195
Kosta Boda, 44

L

Lace-Up Shoes, 8, 48–49
Lady Diana, 196
Lamston's Variety Store, 186
Land A-Sale, 176–177
Latham Outlet Village, 71–72
Lazar, Elysa, 18, 19
L.B.C. Clothing, 82–83
Leather Collection, West Side
    Design Center, 153
Leather furniture, 152–153
Lechter's Housewares & Gifts,
    130–131
L'Eggs, 39
Lenox Factory Store, 71
Lesh Clothing Company, 83, 202
Leslies Bootery, 7
Let Them Eat Cake, 175
Lewis & Clark/Explorer's
    Company, 86
Liberty Village, 43–44
Lighthouse for the Blind, The, 78
Lighting, 150–151
    districts for, 11
Lighting Showroom, 150
Lisa Lighting, 150
Little Red Schoolhouse, 28
Liza's Plus Fashions, 71
Liz Claiborne (Woodbury
    Common), 70
Loehmann's, 101
Lo-Price Discount, 117
Lord & Taylor Clearance Center, 77
L'Oreal Beauty Response Center, 116
Lower Fifth Avenue, 202–203
L.S. Clothing, 90–91
Luggage, 50, 136–142
    mail-order, 37
Luggage Plus, 50

M

McDonald's (Woodbury Common), 70
McKay Drugs, 117–118
Macy's, xii
  carpet cleaning, 150
  one-day sales events, 15–16
Macy's of Brooklyn, xii
Madison Avenue, Upper, 198–199
Mad Monk, The, 179
Mail shopping, 30–37, 191–192
M & M Shoe Center, 7–8
Manhattan, address chart for, xiii–xiv
Manhattan Art and Antiques, 12
Manhattan Branch of Century 21, 57, 193
Manhattan Factory Store, 70–71, 73
Mano a Mano, 87, 201
Marburn Curtain Warehouse, 39
Marcus & Company Appraisers, 125–126
Marie's Ceramic World, 65
Mashuguna Ike, 195
Maternity clothes, 34, 96–97
Maternity Warehouse Outlet, 34
MCI, 168–169
Menswear, 81–92
  sample sales, 21
Merns Mart, 84
Merriment Boulevard, 179
Messenger services, 170–171
Metropolitan Museum of Art, 123
Mexx, 106
Mighty Mac Factory Direct Store, 39
Mikasa outlet, 41
Mink Originals, 21
Minnetonka, 6
Mitchell, 45
Modern Hatters, 92
Moe Ginsburg, 89
Money exchanges, 169
Mouse 'N Around, 105
Movie Line, 173
Mr. M's, 119
Ms., Miss, or Mrs., 95–96
Murray Waxman, 202
Museum of Folk Art Gift Shop, 122–123
Museum of Modern Art, 122
Mystic Color Labs, 28, 172

N

Nader Foods, 202
Naga Antiques, 147
Napier Company Factory Store, 125

Nathan Borlam, 107–108
National Computer Exchange, 167
National Council Thrift Mart, 53–54
National Jewelry Mart, 121
National Liquidators Warehouse, 201
N.B.O., 81
New Jersey, 38–44
Newmark & Lewis, 160–161
New York Army-Navy, 82
New York Farm market, 70
New York Furniture Center, leather furniture, 152
New York Shoe Company, 5
New York Sock Mart, 186
New York's Visitor's Bureau, 174
90th Street Pharmacy, 198–199
99X, 3
No Nonsense Brand Names (For Less), 34
Norbert Hairstylists, 115
Norman J. Seaman's Conert Club, 172
Novelties, 178–184
Now Voyager Freelance Couriers, 174–175
N.Y. Gas Lighting Company, 150

O

Off-Broadway show tickets, 13, 188
Olden Camera, Lens, Video & Computer, 161–162
Old Mystic Flea Market, 28
Omanti, 19–20
Once Upon A Time, 104–105
One-day sales events, 15–16
Oneida Factory Store, 72
One Night Stand, 99
Orchard Bootery, 8
Orchard Street, 45–50
  shoes on, 8
Ormont Shoes, 6
Outdoor street sellers. *See* Street vendors
Outerwear, 74–80
Out of Our Drawers, 182

P

Pageant Books, 15
Pandemonium, 94
Paper goods, 127–135
Parent Pending, 96
Parisian Perfumes, 111–112

Parking discounts, 171
Parking Garage, Inc., 171
Parts Unlimited, 194–195
Paterson's Silk, 200
Peninsula Buying Service, 163–164
People's Flowers, 184
Perfume Encounter, 111
Perfume Plus, 41
Perfumes, 110–119
 district for, 10, 111–114
Petak's, 198
Petland Discount, 200
Pet supplies, 200
 mail-order, 36
Phillipson-Chamberts Press, 196
Phone services, 173–174
Photo exchanges, 13
Picasso Hairstylists, 115
Pierre Furs, 80
Piers 88, 90, and 92, 23
Pink Pussycat Boutique, 180
Pintchik Paints, 151
Plants and flowers, 184
 districts for, 11
Plaza on Eighth, 5
Plus II Athlete's Outlet, 40
P. Miller and Son, 76–77
Pocketbooks. *See* Handbags
Poco Poco, 195
Police Department Auctions, 27
Poppins, 195
Post Office Auctions, 27
Pottery Barn, 133
Pottery Barn Warehouse, 133
Previous markdown, 188–189
Price Club, 168
Pricewatchers, 154
Price Wise, Inc., 117
Pro Video Distributors, 31
P.S. 41 Flea Market, 24
Public restrooms, 189
Purses. *See* Handbags
Pushcart/Joblot, The, 25–26, 197

R
Real estate auctions, 176–177
Reborn Maternity, 97
Records, 193
 districts for, 9–10
Record World, 193
Redi-Cut Carpets, 149
Reminiscence, 98
Revlon Professional Products, 116
Rice & Breskin, 107
Richie's children's shoes, 3–4
Ricky's, 117

Ritz Shoe Store, 5
Robbins, 195, 200
Robin Importers, 128–129
Robin's Nest, 108
Rochester, Connecticut, 72–73
Ronlee, 77
Roosevelt Raceway Flea Market, 24
Rosenbaum Jewelry, 70
Rothman's, 83
Royal Doulton outlet
 Flemington, 44
 Woodbury Common, 69
Royal House, 69
Rugs, 148–150
Rug Tower, 149
Rug Warehouse, The, 149
Runner's World, 2

S
St. Luke's Thrift Shop, 98
St. Martin, 20
Sakhi Fabrics, 195
Saks Fifth Avenue, xii
Salem Street mini-marts, 43
Salwen Umbrellas, 134
Sample sales, ix, 17–22
 advance notice, 192
Samples Women's Collection, 43
S & B Report, 18
S & W Ladies Wear, 100
San Salvage Store, 130
Save-A-Thon, 158
Savemart, 200
Seaman's, 199–200
Sears Roebuck (Bronx; Brooklyn),
 xii, xiii
Season price break, xi
Seasonal shopping, xi, 186–187
Second Act, 108
Second Cousin, 181
Second-hand clothing
 districts for, 11
 funky-clothing stores, 15
Service contracts, 166–167
Services, 168–177
Shades of the Village, 182
Sharper Image, The, 160
Sherman Shoes, 7
Sheru Enterprises, 121–122
Ship 'n Shore, 43
Shoes, 1–8
 mail-order, 36
 size charts for, xv
Shopping by mail, 30–37, 191–192
Shortcuts for Kids, 115
Sidewalk sellers. *See* Street vendors

Sid's Hardware, 63–64
Simply Samples, 18
Sixth Avenue Electronics City, 158–159
Sixth Avenue Flea Market, 24, 25–27
Size charts, xiv–xv
S. Klein Kiddie Shop, 107
Sky Reporter, 174
Sleep Hotline, 173
Sock Express, 186
Socks Plus, 69
Soho, Broadway in, 201
Soho Canal Antique Market, 24
Soho Surplus, 82, 201
Soldier Shop, 198
Sotheby's, 27
Sportswear Systems, 40
Standard Equipment, 61–62
Stanley Novak Company, 134
Staples, The Office Superstore, 127–128
Stapleton Shoe counter, 7
Stationery, 127–135
Statuary, The, 72
Stereo/Video Warehouse, 62–63
Steuben Glass Factory, 73
Stocking up, x–xi
Stock sale, ix
Street vendors, 15, 185
  how to shop, 29
Strings, 183
Sunglasses USA, 176
Superior Optical Company, 22
Supermarkets, 187
Surplus store, ix
Sweet Feet, 5
Swiss Sun Tanning Salon, 114
Sym's, 79, 81

T
Tahari, 41
TAMA County Fair, 23
Tel Consumer, 174
Telephone services, 173–174
Tel-Med, 174
That's The Ticket, 175–176
Theater Development Fund (TDF), 188
Theater tickets, 13, 188
Thom McAn, 200
Thrift shops
  districts for, 11–12
  menswear in, 88
  womenswear in, 98–99
Tiffany & Company, 120

Time Trader, 52
TKTS booths, 188
Tobaldini, 47
Tops Appliance City, 166
Tops 'N Bottoms, 39
Totes Factory Outlet, 35, 134
Tower Records, 9
Toy Center, 202
Toy Liquidators, 39
Toyon Leather Shop, 136
Trader, The, 139–140
Trader Horn, 162–163, 200
Trash and Vaudeville, 98
Trevi, 46–47
Trishop Thrift Boutique, 98–99
Turntable Junction, 43–44

U
Umbrellas, 134
Uncle Steve, 157–158
Underworld Plaza, 56
Unique Clothing Warehouse, 97–98
Unique Courier, 171
United Parcel Service (UPS), 175
United Pharmacal Co. (UPCO), 36
United States Apparel, 41
United States Customs Auctions, 173
Upholstered Room, The, 154
Upper Madison Avenue, 198–199
Urban Archeology, 146
Used clothing. *See* Second-hand clothing
Utrecht Manufacturing Company, 62

V
Value Hosiery, 54
V & Q Health and Beauty, 112
Van Heusen Factory Outlet
  Corning, 73
  Harmon Cove Outlet Center, 41
  Latham Outlet Village, 71
  Woodbury Common, 69
Victoria's Secret of London, 37
Victory Shirt Company, 91
Vidal Sassoon, 116
Village Cobbler, 5
Village Fashion Outlet, 43
Village Outlet, 43
Village Tannery, 141
Vim, 200
VIP Mill Stores, 39
Vitamins, 132–133
V. J. Jones, 55–56

W

Waldenvideo by Mail, 31–32
Walter's World Famous Union
    Square Shops, 24
Wamsutta Factory Outlets, 33
Warehouse sales, 191
Warren Street, 196–197
Wavelengths, 115
WBAI Holiday Crafts Fair, 26–27
W.C. Art & Drafting Supply Co., 60
Weinstock & Yaeger, 124
Weiss & Mahoney, 2, 82
Weissman-Heller & Sons, 202
Wendy's Store, 105–106
We Sell Whole Sale, 196
West Eighth Street Shoe Stores, 5
West Side Design Center, Leather
    Collection, The, 153
West Village, 181–182
Whim shopping, 189–190
Whitney Museum of American Art,
    122–123

Whittal & Shon, 96–98
Wholesale Art Group of Morse
    Harris, The, 169
Wholesale only shops, 192
Wholesaler's Shoe Outlet, 3, 41
Wicker furniture, 151–152
Wickery, The, 152
Willingboro Mall, 42
Windsore Shirt Company, 43
WilliWear, 41
Wiz, The, 165–166
Womenswear, 93–103
    sample sales, 17–22
Woodbury Common, 68–71
Woolworth, 200
World Couriers of Queens, 175
Wright's Barn Flea Market, 28

Y

Year in sale days, xv–xvi
Yorkville Flea Market, 24–25
Young's Hats, 91–92

BARGAIN COUPONS

These coupons come from a variety of establishments: Some are stores, others are services, and still others are entertainment spots. These are one-time offers given to readers of *Bargain Hunting in Greater New York*. Tear them out one by one, and, if my description wasn't enough, you will have an additional incentive to visit a new store or make use of a new service. Hopefully, the coupon will initiate a gratifying customer-vendor relationship. Who knows? You might get this special discount each time you come by.

AIDA'S AND JIMI'S MERCHANDISING CO.
41 West 28th Street, 2nd Floor
New York, NY 10001
689-2415

☞ *5 percent off wholesale price*

Famous children's and ladies' wholesale to the retail public

ASTOR PLACE
2 Astor Place
New York, NY 10003
475-9854

☞ *10 percent off any services*

Great haircuts for great people

THE AUCTION REPORT
112 East 36th Street
New York, NY 10016
679-5400

☞ *15% off subscription; normally $35, now $30*

All the advertised and unadvertised auctions, shows, and fairs

BABYTOES CLOTHING
High Street, Box 522
Phoenicia, NY 12464
914/688-7922
Note: Babytoes clothing is sold on the sidewalk at
Prince & West Broadway daily. Or write for price list.

☞ *$2 off all baby clothing*

Hand-painted clothing for babies and infants

BARNES & BARNES FINE FURNITURE
190 Commerce Avenue
Southern Pines, NC 28387
800/334-8174

☞ *10 percent off*

Special-order buying makes $ense

BASKETS AND BLADES UNLIMITED
Norwalk Factory Outlet
11 Rowan Street
East Norwalk, CT 06855
203/838-1349

☞ *10 percent off any merchandise*

BILL BEECHER
Contractor
244 West 56th Street
New York, NY 10019
581-4793

☞ *Wood floors—sanding and refinishing—$20 off the job*

BIMINI TWIST RESTAURANT
345 Amsterdam Avenue
New York, NY 10024
362-1260

☞ *10 percent discount on food (no beverage)*

A kinder gentler version of the beer-and-burger joint

BLACK WATER
A variety of cassettes, CDs, collections, postcards, and art
514 Washington Street
Hoboken, NJ 07030
201/656-3438

☞ *15 percent off any merchandise*

The impossible breaking into the possible

THE BRASS LOFT
499 Broadway
New York, NY 10012
226-5467

Expires 12/31/91
See Manager

☞ *30 percent discount on fireplace equipment*

Largest selection of brass giftware, fireplace furnishings, etc.

THE CANDLE SHOP
118 Christopher Street
New York, NY 10014
989-0148

Expires 12/31/91
See Manager

☞ *10 percent off any merchandise*

Largest array of candles in New York

CAPEZIO DANCE-THEATER SHOP
177 MacDougal Street
New York, NY 10014
477-5634

Expires 12/31/91
See Manager

☞ *10 percent discount*

**Internationally recognized store for dance, theater, fitness
gear**

THE CAPEZIO STORE
1650 Broadway at 51st Street, 2nd floor
New York, NY 10019
245-2130

☞ *10 percent off*

The one place for dance and theater clothing

CHELSEA FRAMES
194 Eighth Avenue
New York, NY 10011
807-8957

☞ *$10 off complete custom framing*

Fine custom framing, antique prints, contemporary posters

CHERRY HILL FURNITURE, CARPET AND INTERIORS
P.O. Box 7405
High Point, NC 27264
800/328-0933

☞ *10 percent off all merchandise (free brochure)*

50 years experience, 500 finest brands

CHILDREN'S MUSEUM OF MANHATTAN
212 West 83rd Street
New York, NY 10019
721-1223

☞ *$1 discount on admission*

Participatory exhibits and activity centers for children ages 2–12 years

CHOCK CATALOG
4 Orchard Street
New York, NY 10002
473-1929

☞ *No charge for catalog*

A diversified selection of hosiery, underwear, bathing suits, and pajamas

CHOCOLATE FACTORY
93 Chambers Street
New York, NY 10007
964-6829

☞ *10 percent off any merchandise*

No better sweets in the world

CIRCLE REPERTORY
99 Seventh Avenue South
New York, NY 10014
924-7100

☞ *50 percent off single ticket price with this coupon depending on ticket availability*

A national resource of new plays

THE CLOTHESWORKS
Norwalk Factory Outlet
11 Rowan Street
East Norwalk, CT 06855
203/838-1349

☞ *10 percent off any merchandise*

Don't be owing your soul to the company store

JEAN COCTEAU REPERTORY
330 Bowery
New York, NY 10012
677-0060

☞ *15 percent off subscription for four plays*

The classic choice

THE COMIC STRIP
1568 Second Avenue
New York, NY 10028
861-9386

☞ *No cover but 2-drink minimum (this is a $7–$12 savings)*

New York's largest showcase comedy club

CSC REPERTORY, CLASSIC STAGE
136 East 13th Street
New York, NY 10003
677-4210

☞ *Purchase one ticket, get a second one free*

A non-profit theater dedicated to innovative productions of classics

---

CUTTING EDGE GRAPHICS
Computer graphics and illustration
510 East 20th Street
New York, NY 10009
353-8790

☞ *15 percent off logo or other design work*

Designing man

D & A MERCHANDISE
22 Orchard Street
New York, NY 10003
925-4766

Expires 12/31/91
See Manager

☞ *10 percent off any merchandise*

We are the original underwear king

DEMBITZER BROTHERS
Electrical appliances
5 Essex Street
New York, NY 10002
254-1310

Expires 12/31/91
See Manager

☞ *10 percent off*

One of the oldest discount houses on the lower east side

MARK DeMURO FINE ART APPRAISER
2350 Broadway
New York, NY 10024
877-2610

Expires 12/31/91
See Manager

☞ *10 percent off appraising of graphics, paintings, and sculptures*

Find out what your art is worth

FARM AND GARDEN NURSERY
2 Avenue of the Americas
New York, NY 10013
431-3577

Expires 12/31/91
See Manager

☞ *10 percent off any live materials*

Manhanttan's largest garden center

FENWICK MEN'S CLOTHES—FACTORY SHOWROOM
22 West 19th Street
New York, NY 10011
243-1100

Expires 12/31/91
See Manager

☞ *Buy any suit and get a fine silk tie FREE!*

Once you shop Fenwick . . . you'll never pay retail again

FINE & KLEIN
119 Orchard Street
New York, NY 10002
674-6720

Expires 12/31/91
See Manager

☞ *30 percent off*

Handbags and small leather goods

FOREMOST FURNITURE SHOWROOMS
8 West 30th Street
New York, NY 10001
889-6347

Expires 12/31/91
See Manager

☞ *15 percent off selected merchandise*

Largest discount furniture showroom in New York—all name brands

---

GEMINI PAPER GOODS
449 Third Street
Park Slope, NY 11215
718/768-5568

Expires 12/31/91
See Manager

☞ *20 percent off any merchandise*

Great gifts to dress up your party

ZINA HASHIMOTO SKIN CARE
123 East 54th Street, Suite 3-D
New York, NY 10022
753-1306

Expires 12/31/91
See Manager

☞ *20 percent discount on balanced natural skin care products*

Paris, Tokyo, New York background

HEAD OVER HEELS
**11 Rowan Street
East Norwalk, CT 06855
203/838-1349**

☛ *$5 dollars off—no limit on purchases (shoes $25 and up)*

Women's name-brand, all-leather fashion shoes

JONATHAN HERZOG
**Real Estate Law Specialist
1015 Madison Avenue
New York, NY 10021
794-2718**

☛ *5 percent off fees*

Extremely competitive fees

INDIAN CAFE
**201 West 95th Street
New York, NY 10025
222-1600**

☛ *25 percent discount Sunday to Thursday only*

A dining experience in Indian cuisine

INTIMATE OUTLET
696 West Avenue
Norwalk, CT 06850
203/853/6939

Expires 12/31/91
See Manager

☞ *$5 off bras and girdles*

Lingerie for every need

JANOVIC/PLAZA INC.
1150 Third Avenue
New York, NY 10021
772-1400

Expires 12/31/91
See Manager

☞ *50 percent discount from true list of Levolor blinds*

Best prices, service on paint, wallcovering, window treatment

---

JOLI TRAVEL AGENCY
49 Park Avenue
New York, NY 10016
213-3396

Expires 12/31/91
See Manager

☞ *20 percent off tours*

Please go away

KAUFMAN LINGERIE
73 Orchard Street
New York, NY 10002
226-1629

Expires 12/31/91
See Manager

☞ *10 percent off any merchandise*

Designer lingerie at wonderful discounts

LAMBRO COMPANY
P.O. Box 161 N
Roslyn, NY 11576
516/883-4629

Expires 12/31/91
See Manager

☞ *10 percent off natural color sweater kit (fishermen's net style)*

First quality wool yarn direct from overseas

LET THEM EAT CAKE
287 Hudson Street
New York, NY 10013
989-4970

Expires 12/31/91
See Manager

☞ *10 percent off any cakes or confectionaries*

LISS OF NORWALK
Norwalk Factory Outlet Center
11 Rowan Street
Norwalk Ct 06855
203/838-1349

 $5 off purchases over $25

Everything for the family

LONE STAR ROADHOUSE
240 West 52nd Street
New York, NY 10019
245-2950

15 percent off any lunch or dinner

A Texas roadhouse in the heart of New York

L. S. CLOTHING
19 West 44th Street, #403
New York, NY 10036
575-0933

6 percent off any merchandise

Finest names in traditional menswear

MANHATTAN GIFTS
314 West 53rd Street
New York, NY 10019
517-1017

☞ *25 percent off on full line of advertising products (promotional items) and if you buy in large quantity, 40 percent*

Advertising and imprinting

MAREL
6 Bond Street
Great Neck, NY 11021
516/466-3118

☞ *10 percent off china, crystal, and giftware*

Since 1963, Marel has serviced customers from coast to coast

MARLO FLOWERS
421 East 73rd Street
New York, NY 10021
628-2246

☞ *15 percent off any merchandise*

Magnificent flowers

RANDY MATUSOW PHOTOGRAPHY
Family and individual portraits, publicity shots,
weddings, and special occasions
118 Third Place
Brooklyn, NY 11231
718/625-2071

☞ *15 percent off any services*

The not-ready-for-wax-museum style of photography

McKAY DRUGS
307 Sixth Avenue (and all other locations)
New York, NY 10014
627-2300

☞ *$3 off any new prescription*

Every day is savings day at McKay

MINNETONKA
P.O. Box 444
Bronx, NY 10458
364-7033

☞ *20 percent off merchandise*

The finest in moccasins and casual footwear

MOOD INDIGO
181 Prince Street
New York, NY 10012
254-1176

☞ *10 percent off any merchandise*

Best selection of art deco collectibles and fiesta in New York

MULTIPLE PERSONALITY
457 West 57th Street
New York, NY 10019
582-8879
page 21
Rocklin, CA 95677
916/624-5718

☞ *20 percent off on weekdays and 15 percent off on weekends*

A multi-faceted approach to perception helping people slow down, remove tension, and improve vision

LEE MYLES TRANSMISSIONS
14 West End Avenue
New York, NY 10023
246-9060

☞ *10 percent off parts and labor*

NATALIE'S WORDS
39 Regent Street
North Plainfield, NJ 07060
201/668-0394

☞ *10 percent off any word processing services*

Your words, my style: light editing too

NATIONAL IMPROVISATIONAL THEATER
223 Eighth Avenue
New York, NY 10011
243-7224

☞ *10 percent off regular performance*

The best in improvisational theater

Native's Guide to New York, **by Richard Laermer**
PRIMA PUBLISHING
P.O. Box 1260 RL
Rocklin, CA 95677
916/624/5718

☞ *10 percent off the guidebook for New Yorkers*

750 ways to have the time of your life in the city

NATURAL GOURMET COOKERY SCHOOL
48 West 21st Street
New York, NY 10010
645-5170

☞ *10 percent discount, Friday night dinner club*

**Health-supportive whole foods cuisine—and it tastes
wonderful**

NEW YORK ASTROLOGY CENTER
545 Eighth Avenue
New York, NY 10018
947-3609

☞ *$5 off horoscope reading*

We do complete personality profiles

NEW YORK YARN CENTER
1011 Sixth Avenue
New York, NY 10018
719-5648

☞ *30 percent off any merchandise*

**Magnificent fashion yarns and needlecraft all at closeout
prices**

NORBERT HAIRSTYLISTS
16 East Eighth Street
New York, NY 10003
473-1330

 Haircut for coupon holders $12.50, and manicure $6

NOW VOYAGER FREELANCE COURIERS
74 Varick Street
New York, NY 10013
431-1616

 $4.50 savings on signup fee for new travel couriers

Dinner in Paris? Now you can!—by flying courier

KATHY O'NEIL, MASSEUSE
29 East 10th Street
New York, NY 10010
777-0810

 10 percent off

Why knot? Massage

ONE NIGHT STAND
905 Madison Avenue
New York, NY 10021
772-7720

☞ *10 percent off rental of a dress*

Elegant dresses from leading designers offered for rent

ORCHARD BOOTERY
75 Orchard Street
New York, NY 10002
966-0688

☞ *25 percent off any merchandise*

Ladies' shoes, boots, and slippers—all at a discount

OUT OF OUR DRAWERS
184 Seventh Avenue South
New York, NY 10014
929-4473

☞ *10 percent off any jewelry*

Expert ear piercing—your choice: with or without pain

Expires 12/31/91
See Manager

PERFORMANCE TRUCKING
Office, Home, and Fine Art Transportation
481 Broadway
New York, NY 10003
677-2332

☞ *15 percent off*

. . . Because the show must go on

Expires 12/31/91
See Manager

PICASSO HAIRCUTTERS
150 Fifth Avenue
New York, NY 10011
206-9004

☞ *25 percent off any service*

Let us create a new you today

Expires 12/31/91
See Manager

PIERRE FURS
224 West 30th Street
New York, NY 10001
244-3790

☞ *$20 off any remodel*

Bring in your old fur coat and we'll bring it back to life with
new style

POSEIDON CONFECTIONARY
629 Ninth Avenue
New York, NY 10036
757-6173

👉 *10 percent off any merchandise*

Oldest Greek bakery in New York City

POST HORN
Norwalk Factory Outlet
11 Rowan Street
East Norwalk, CT 06855
203/838-1349

👉 *$5 off women's designer clothing purchases*

ROBIN IMPORTERS
510 Madison Avenue
New York, NY 10022
753-6475

👉 *10 percent off any merchandise*

Affordable elegance on name-brand tabletop lines

ROGER ROTH AND DAVE
123 Seventh Avenue
New York, NY 10011
989-1184

☞ *$1 off any purchase*

Cards, tees & toys

ROTHSCHILD/MOSS
Marketing Consultants to New Businesses
P.O. Box 6117
New York, NY 10150
832-2052

☞ *$100 off first consultation*

Careful planning + innovative techniques = success

RUPPERT'S
1662 Third Avenue
New York, NY 10128
831-1900

☞ *One free entrée with purchase of another of equal or greater value*

A restaurant/bar serving regional American specialties

ST. LUKE'S THRIFT SHOP
487 Hudson Street
New York, NY 10014
924-9364

☞ *20 percent off any merchandise*

We sell everything (well, almost) including furniture

S & B REPORT
112 East 36th Street
New York, NY 10016
679-5400

☞ *15 percent discount on one-year subscription,*
normally $40; with coupon, $34

Passport to designer showroom sales

JEAN PIERRE SAND SKIN CARE
P.O. Box 263
Riverdale, NY 10471

☞ *Free $60 perfume gift with any $50 purchase*

Luxury for less

S & W LADIES WEAR
165 West 26th Street
New York, NY 10001
924-6656

☞ *10 percent off everything, including all markdowns*

**Complete current designer women's fashion at a discount of
25–50 percent**

SEAMAN'S CONCERT/THEATER CLUB
130 St. Edward's Street, #7-A
Brooklyn, NY 11201
718/855-9293

☞ *$11.20 discount off regular price of membership*

**Free Off-Broadway, Carnegie, and Lincoln Center—
Broadway tix at just $2**

☞ *Double cassette for $13/CD for $17—save $3 off
regular price*

**"THE '70S PRESERVATION SOCIETY PRESENTS
THOSE FABULOUS SEVENTIES"**
60 Third Avenue
New York, NY 10003
473-9173

☞ *Double cassette for $13 / CD for $17—save $3 off
regular price*

One volume of 23 *unforgettable* top 10 hits of the 1970s

SHADES OF THE VILLAGE
167 Seventh Avenue South
New York, NY 10014
255-7767

 10 percent off any sunglasses

Best selection/price in New York City

SHAKESPEARE & COMPANY
2259 Broadway
New York, NY 10024
580-7800

15 percent off any merchandise

SHOP BY MAIL
112 East 36th Street
New York, NY 10016
679-5400

$3 off—normally $18 for four issues; with coupon, $15

Hardly known discount sales by mail

STAND-UP NEW YORK
236 West 78th Street
New York, NY 10024
595-0850

☞ *No cover charge ($7–$12 savings)*

A top comedy headline club

STANLEY MOSS CORPORATE GRAPHIC DESIGN
Specializing in corporate identity and publication
design
336 East 53rd Street
New York, NY 10022
924-3041

☞ *$100 off first consultation*

Corporate graphic design for the global arena

STEP BY STEP DANCE INSTRUCTION
410 Riverside Drive
New York, NY 10024
678-5958

☞ *$25 off any private lesson: wolf and fox-trot, tango, cha-cha, mambo, merengue, swing, waltz, and lindy to couples, singles*

The world is my dance floor

TALLER LATINOAMERICANO
63 East Second Street
New York, NY 10003
777-2250

 10 percent off any Spanish or Portuguese language class

Learn Spanish in an atmosphere of cultural promiscuity

TENDER BUTTONS
143 East 62nd Street
New York, NY 10021
758-7004

10 percent off any merchandise

TERRE GRAFF
16 East 55th Street
New York, NY 10024
206-4014

10 percent off designer clothing

European and American designer fashions at a 75–85% discount

THEATER IN OUR TIME
335 West 19th Street
New York, NY 10011
929-6019

☞ *$3 off any ticket*

Broadway and Off-Broadway salons with the stars

TIDY ST. JOHN SALON SPA
435 East 86th Street
New York, NY 10028
534-7600

☞ *20 percent off Sunday, Monday, and Tuesday only
(plus free $25 kit of shampoos, etc.)*

You deserve the best today

WHITTALL AND SHON
247 West 37th Street
New York, NY 10018
594-2626

☞ *10 percent off current merchandise*

Sample sale on hats, silk scarves, and all sportswear

Klaus Walter

- painter
- track lighting
- pisos
  <u>tile kitchen</u>.

done early July
(1st or 2nd).

- george ortiz
- claus.
  monday 9:30.

change sink.

- Ana
- Brazil — 011-5511-253 441
- Mex.nt: 1 hr. earlier.

- access call → call #
   voz; dial 111 ;   6   mensages
   nuevos.

   play new 6
   all   7
   repeat   2
   skip fwd 5
   # help.

_____

   Sears -
   Plaza las Americas
   ↳ 258-2798
809-258-2798
   8-68775-75988-9
   Rebecca-   514-720-1577
        FRI AM